NARCISSISTIC EX:

HOW TO RECOGNIZE EMOTIONAL ABUSE IN INTIMATE RELATIONSHIPS, GET OVER IT AND STOP BEING CONTROLLED BY MANIPULATIVE PEOPLE.

Table of Contents

Introduction

Recognizing the Narcissist is a guide that focus mainly on explaining all the possible ways that can be used to identify if a narcissist is present in your life (it can be a parent, your partner or any other person); the book gives you also practical tips on how to cope with their potentially toxic behavior and the ways you can get free from manipulation.

A narcissist is a person who suffers from a disorder known as narcissistic personality disorder, a mental disorder whereby the sufferer has an exaggerated sense of self-importance, lack empathy for others, and a deep need for admiration. Although narcissistic individuals might seem oddly confident, they have a very fragile sense of self-esteem and often take offense to the slightest of criticism.

Historically, the word 'narcissism' originates from Greek mythology, specifically the myth of Narcissus, a physically attractive hunter who was so proud of his looks that he ignored the people around him. At one time, as he was looking at his reflection in a pond, he fell in love with it. The gods ended up punishing him for this act and he eventually died.

Narcissism is a concept that draws its roots from psychoanalytic theory; its spot in the limelight started in 1914 when Sigmund Freud wrote an essay about it. A person suffering from the narcissistic personality disorder can experience many negative issues in different areas of their life. If you work with, go to school with, or are in a relationship with a narcissist, you may experience difficulties dealing with this individual.

The truth is not all narcissists are the same! Thus, let's learn about the different types of narcissists first!

So sit back and enjoy as we read all about narcissism.

Chapter 1: Flying Monkeys

So what is meant by the term Flying Monkeys in the context of narcissism? So Flying Monkeys are essentially agents of the narcissists. People who carry out requests or some kind of order made by a narcissist. Sometimes because they have to. Like in an employment situation. If the narcissist is their boss. Some because they want to, so they may be sadistic or share the same goal and some because they are manipulated into doing so. Now in chronicle practice we use the term agents instead of flying monkeys and there are a few reasons for this. So you may be thinking that one of the reasons is that we tend to avoid colloquial terms and this is correct but there are actually a couple of reasons as well.

The main reason we use agents instead of Flying Monkeys is the age of the reference. So the flying monkey reference goes back to the movie "The Wizard of Oz" that was released in 1939. And you can even say further back to a book written in the 1900s "The Wonderful Wizard of Oz" which called the characters Winged Monkeys not Flying Monkeys. So because both of those references are of course quite old. I noticed that most people don't get them. They have never seen the movie or if they did see the movie they don't remember the winged monkeys.

Now the last reason we use agents instead of the term Flying Monkeys is that because in the movie, the 1939 movie The Wizard of Oz. The Winged Monkeys didn't talk and it wasn't clear why they followed orders. The orders issued by the wicked witch of the West. So intent is really an important facid of the narcissistic agent construct. So if we don't know the intent, that really makes it confusing, makes it harder to figure out what the Flying Monkey or the Agent is up to. Now interestingly, in the book the Winged Monkeys were forced to follow orders because of a spell that was attached to this golden cap. And the Winged Monkeys had the spell casted upon them because they threw a prince in a river. So there is a lot to it, so they were mischievous Winged Monkeys and they got into some trouble. And whoever had this golden cap could issue them three orders. So they would work for anyone who had it. They were not necessarily loyal to anyone specifically and in the book they were eventually freed from the spell. So in the narcissist uses of Flying Monkeys or Agents, what to the agents do? Well this depends on situation but they can carry out a variety of orders or requests like we mentioned before. So they can just generally support the narcissist so they can be on the side of the narcissist little to them despite the destructive nature of narcissism. They can echo the message of the narcissist so they can act and furtherance of gas lighting so they can say the same thing as the narcissist to manipulate the narcissist usually romantic partner into believing that they are the problem so their romantic partner will believe that they are the problem.

So this is really gas lighting by proxy. They can spread about the narcissist partner and this makes the narcissist seem more credible because now more than one person is saying the same lie. But also it makes the partner of the narcissist feel like they have less worth. Rumors are damaging which of course is something that narcissist typically want to happen to their partner. They want their partners to feel like they have less value or like they are worthless. By putting the partner down, the narcissist feels like they are moving up. The agents can simply be sent to harass or demean the partner of the narcissist. Sometimes these behaviors are not really complex. So they can just go and harass somebody and cause trouble directly like that. They can be sent to encourage you to make up with the narcissist like after the argument. So they might say "Hey give him another chance. They're really not a bad person. They're really not narcissistic. There is a big misunderstand." So really kind of try to negotiate in behalf of the narcissist. Now interestingly they can also be sent to support you around the same goal of the narcissist. So they can seem like they are on your side, they might give you someone to talk to, to vent to, about the bad behavior of the narcissist but really they still have the same agenda in mind. Which of course they share with the narcissist. So in essence they can be sent to make peace. They can also be sent to apologize something narcissist typically have a lot of trouble doing directly but they may do by proxy. So the agent might come off very convincing, remorseful, kind of all the characteristics you wish you could see in the partner that is narcissistic. You'll see it in the agent but not on the narcissist. And this can still lead to someone being convinced or they can still be persuasive because there is this idea that the narcissist had these feelings they expressed them to the agent. And you're really seen through that agent so it makes the narcissist seem a little bit more endearing.

Another way of course you could look at it is by the narcissist using an agent to do that work that's very destructive and not good communication. So there's two ways to look at this particular type of manipulation or just direction given to the agent. Similarly, I've also seen agents sent in situations where the narcissist has been cut off by their partner in a more dramatic and definitive way. So the victim says they won't communicate with narcissist anymore there is no talking at all. And here's where you see the agent show up out of nowhere. So not having any contact any communication with the narcissist. It's kind of a powerful position. Narcissist doesn't like that loss of control so again agents tend to be sent right after that type of decisions make.

Now agents can do other things as well, these are just some of the common behaviors for the agent.

Chapter 2: Narcissistic Stalking

We all have a proper to feel secure as we go about our day by day lives. Stalking is a criminal offense and ought to no longer be taken lightly. Serious instances of stalking may additionally result in a target living in a kingdom of fear, having to depart their home or work or in excessive cases, death. Justice structures in many components of the world have failed in figuring out and managing the dangers involved. Why?

A lack of information and understanding of what goes on inner the thoughts of a stalker and inadequate training. Being stalked is considered one of the maximum terrifying things we can revel in from a narcissist. I absolutely get how shattered, violated and scared you feel in case you are going through the horror of this proper now. Being stalked, or even the danger of stalking incites feeling agoraphobic about going everywhere or doing anything in case the narcissist is following you. You don't recognize where she or he should turn up and what drama could ensue.

What is Stalking?

Stalking is expressed as unaccepted and obsessive attention through a person or persons closer to another individual. This may also include following or spying on their target or monitoring them by means of any way consisting of social media. This can also without delay or indirectly talk a risk to the sufferer or instil fear or distress onto their sufferer.

The maximum commonplace form of stalking can be taken into consideration obsessional, where the stalker is a former associate who will now not take delivery of that the connection is over. This is usually preceded by way of some form of abuse inside the dating and is regularly practiced by way of people with a character disorder and people with controlling personalities. This particular sort of stalking is achieving epidemic proportions in today's society and is unfortunately, now not constantly taken seriously via law enforcement agencies.

Maybe, you sense completely fearful approximately having any social media accounts. Maybe you realize that the narcissist has used strategies and people to hack into your statistics or discover information about you to use in opposition to you or terrorize and dismantle your life.

Some people may let you know to threaten a narcissist returned to forestall them stalking you or attempt to expose them and convey them into accountability. In stark contrast, I even have seen human beings trying to get even and 'one-up' the narcissist come off distinctly badly due to the fact no level of doing so that it will ever be powerful when we're coming from the inner emotional box of trauma. Of course, the chance of something like that is terrifying. All of this is specifically terrible when we realize that we're dealing with jealousy, controlling narcissists. These are the ones who're the maximum in all likelihood to be vindictive, poisonous and even risky.

And I also get how after being stalked and no longer understanding whether or not or not we are being — that we may be in constant paranoia questioning if we nevertheless are being stalked. We don't realize whether it's far safe to come returned out and if we do what is going to be fed to others, used against us in a courtroom or flung in our face. Or if joint-parenting, how the stalking of our facts can be used in opposition to us with our children or incite similarly abusive interrogation of our children.

Additionally, you could suspect the folks who come and see you or speak to you are clearly minions of the narcissist. Gang stalking may be a completely actual phenomenon with narcissists, whereby their memories approximately you have got incited other humans to cyber stalk and bully you or attack you in your normal life operations. And all of this could loaf around for years making your existence sense terrorized, faded and substantially unsafe. I promise you until I had located the answer to this, I too might be completely minimalized. In reality, I know I could by no means have survived.

Sadly, victims are frequently permitted down by the crook justice process with their reports not taken significantly and treated accordingly. Traditionally narcissists feed off your strength as a shark does blood and get energized to assault you. There is a much better way to triumph over the narcissist's stalking.

Meaning, heal to the empowered degree where you have the healthy beliefs 'all of the lifestyles help me' and 'my radiant, authentic self is impervious to abuse – just due to being myself.'

People ask me often as to whether or now not I am perturbed approximately the ex-narcissists stalking me online. Both of those men were very vindictive guys – however the truth is I don't care if they look my stuff up constantly or now not at all. I'm now not concerned approximately them having a crack at me, or any narcissist having a cross at me for that matter. Because there may be simply an easy philosophy – forget about the nasty behavior and if a boundary is crossed – simply implement it. This approach to block a person who is being abusive or take out an intervention order if necessary.

Stalking is a totally lots underreported crime yet, it has an exquisite impact on those who have been the sufferer of such against the law. It has to be referred to that stalking is not restricted to romantic relationships however may consist of friends and co-workers.

Why Do Narcissists Stalk?

Have you spotted them lurking close to your place of work or your home? Are they invading your privacy? Normal people be given whilst dating is over and doesn't display up at places in which they expect you to be. You had been as soon as underneath their manipulation and they want to hold it that way. They experience entitled to your interest, the narcissistic deliver they received from you and the electricity they had over you. One of the narcissist's biggest fears is losing someone who they had complete manipulation over.

The truth which you have called, 'time' for your dating is of no significance to them. You have been once their puppet to be performed with as they saw the match and they nonetheless want to have manipulated these strings. Their envy of you being able to enjoy lifestyles without them often becomes pathological. They are green with envy of the qualities which you possess that they realize they can never have, together with your empathy, excessive morals and integrity.

Your rejection of them cuts them to their very core. 'How dare you reject me… I'm the one who does the rejecting… If I can't have you, no-one else will.' Just due to the fact the relationship is over, doesn't mean that their want for manage has ended. This isn't all about power and manipulates, however approximately 'ownership.' Even if the narcissist has moved on and observed another character to govern and dominate, they don't need to look you shifting on looking to be a huge part of your existence for all of your existence.

This sort of behaviour is psychotically practiced through a person who's genuinely delusional, jealous and probably insecure. A stalker may be dangerous going to extreme lengths to preserve on to a person who they may be afraid to permit go of. They don't want you to transport on and find someone else.

Emotional stalkers have a basic want to rid themselves of prevailing emptiness. They frequently obtain this by carefully deciding on a sufferer who is then charmed, seduced and trapped. The victim's strength feeds the stalker and gives what he lacks.

Being incapable of love, these narcissistic stalkers are ravaged by the livid envy they sense for those who truly revel in existence. We're not speaking of material assets, however of moral qualities: vitality, empathy, sensitivity, creativity, goals, and lifestyle projects. Besides, they're now not so clean to identify. They can without difficulty transfer their mind-set from being charming and caring, to being ruthlessly vital and dismissive, feeding the victim's confusion and self-doubt.

Emotional stalkers are successful in captivating their friends and family with their wit, leaving their victims feeling even extra bewildered with their reputedly innocent but really aggressive and humiliating jokes.

Narcissist stalkers often search for these common traits in victims:

Underlying Low Self-Esteem: Victims of emotional stalkers crave acknowledgement from their companion, although forever doubting their worthiness of it. This is what makes them vulnerable.

Above Average Intelligence: Emotional stalkers are seeking for very intelligent, honestly bright, quite skilled, well-trained victims. They look for enthusiasm and ardour about their career.

Good Work Ethic and Personal Accountability: Stalkers search for their victims to be very accountable and difficult workers, constantly complying with a first rate fulfilment of obligations assigned.

Extreme Perfectionists: Victims have a tendency to accept as true with nothing they do is ever correct enough, all the time striving to acquire acknowledgement, meanwhile doubting their real worth.

Dependable and Always Ready to Help Others: Victims tend to keep a low profile and haven't any wish to overshadow friends or work colleagues.

What Motivates a Stalker?

Stalkers may start their harassment by using time and again calling or contacting their goal through email and social media however it doesn't always quit there. If those techniques of touch are ineffective "the man or woman may also improve to greater intrusive behaviors consisting of spying on, and suddenly confronting their sufferers," stated Robert T. Muller in his article, Mind of a Stalker.

In many cases, stalking begins at the quilt of courting, however, there may be no perfect technology to determine who will or won't grow to be a stalker. But, thanks to researchers we now understand motivating elements that power some humans to stalk. These factors encompass:

Rejection: Whether the rejection is real or simply perceived by the stalker it comes as an important blow. Stalkers see themselves as the sufferers of being led on or toyed with. Their worry of abandonment doesn't permit them to reason, so it's impossible to allow them to down smoothly.

Obsession: Stalkers are often obsessive in multiple areas of their existence including their romantic inclinations. They generally have repetitive concept patterns that play like a broken record, in order that they gradually become so preoccupied with their target, they're not able to sleep, neglect to eat, and permit their jobs to visit the wayside.

Fantasy: Stalkers blur the strains between reality and fiction. They harbor a feel of entitlement that their objectives belong to them which feeds the delusion that they're destined to be together. Some come to be so convinced, they'll invent information of their head about a romantic dating that doesn't exist, and that they'll be so sure of it, they're capable of persuading others.

Narcissism: Stalkers are not able to understand or appreciate the emotions or boundaries of others. They also lack wholesome coping abilities to address rejection, embarrassment, shame, or loss. This becomes particularly problematic if you formerly had a romantic dating as they will justify their moves with "If I'm suffering, so have to you" good judgment or the "If I can't have you, no one can."

How do you reply to the narcissistic stalker?

You have got to set company barriers and permit your stalker to understand that you will no longer tolerate this shape of harassment. Let them know that you may have no hesitation related to the regulation and that you'll record them to the best authorities if necessary. If they fail to recognize and abide by using your wishes to be left alone, name the police. No touch is vitally im2345portant whilst leaving a dating with a narcissist.

When all attempts at making contact with you have got failed, a narcissist can also use your youngsters as a means of having the desired result. Stalking is perhaps pleasant understood by means of each the stalker and their victim with buddies, relatives and law enforcement regularly not taking the scenario critically, unfortunately sometimes, with tragic results.

Chapter 3: Stories of People Who Experienced a Toxic Relationship

A Narcissistic Relationship (Story)

Let me tell you a story of how a friend survived a narcissistic relationship (marriage) she was in for a couple of years.

As a little girl, one of my favorite fairy tale movies was Cinderella. This was before I was able to think logically. Then, I could envision my life with the man of my dreams, my prince charming that would rescue me from the present state. What became a problem was the fact that I carried on this thought until my late twenties. Before then, my situation, which I thought was terrible and needed saving was not actually what it was in the real sense. Though I was hooked to such dream, it was no surprise to me or anyone who knew me when I fell head over heels with little brain work, which was supposed to be my fairy godmother to the one man who came to me as a prince charming. There was no one to tell me to hold on or to ask me to give it a second thought. I could not even think for myself. Instead, I dived right into a relationship with him.

As always, it was all rosy; he said the right things, did the right things, showered me with the most beautiful things, and made me feel like a princess. Though Cinderella fell in love with the right prince charming, I thought I had done the same. I thought I had hit the jackpot. I did not even attempt to try out the silver shoe to be sure it fitted me right.

The necessary steps were not taken. If I told anyone this story, they would give me a knock on the head. Within weeks of knowing each other and dating, he professed his love to me, and I all but agreed. I blushed to the tip of my toes when he told me I was everything he had been praying for, everything he wished for, and more. What was going through my mind during that period was I had met my soul mate, and no one could tell me otherwise.

He played his part so well that I did not suspect anything.

As I said before, I did not bother to think or ask questions to be sure I was making the right choice; after all, he said I was THE ONE. Well, he could not keep his eyes and hands off me. We did what anyone in love would do. We had healthy sex — more like almost - every day in a week - sex. He wrote love letters to me, sang love songs to me, lavished me with gifts, and was always taking me out every weekend and whatnot. What made my heart pound ever so often was the fact that he promised to make me the mother of his unborn children and his wife. After that, there was nothing I could do but to enjoy the love ride with my eyes shut. It was frightening, but I enjoyed every day of it.

Sometimes, we tend to say "had I known" when we realize that we are in a very uncomfortable situation. We wish we could predict the future before diving into something, but when the going is excellent, we do not see things that way.

Everything about my prince charming was perfect; in fact, he was the ideal man for me. All of him was perfect. He knew every inch of me, my likes and dislikes, my favorite songs, my favorite dishes, my favorite color, my favorite everything. He had every quality a woman would sort after in a man. Every suspicion that was growing in me was drowned every time he talked about how fate brought us together. He says the right things every time.

After marriage, it turned out that my fairy tale script was not following the right order. I made myself believe that he was going through rough patches, and he would come through eventually. Little did I know that that was just the beginning of my problems. Despite everything, I still tried to perform my wifely duties. I was loyal, committed, was always at his beck and call. I opened myself to him. I let him have everything from me; my love, my kindness, my care, my understanding, my humility, my forgiveness, hoping everything would change.

Well, everything changed…

…for the worse.

I was still forgiving and understanding. If I had not, I would be paying attention to every red flag, and I would then try to call him to order. Sometimes, I sit and analyze everything that is happening and beginning to question my judgments. I saw the warning signs, but whenever he seems to be remorseful about them, I turn a blind eye; but it persists.

I remember in the past, when he does something that is not acceptable, he owns up and sometimes become teary-eyed, and I become very soft and forgiving when that happens. I realized a little bit late that it was his way of getting away from things. He would seem so helpless that you would have nothing to do but to sympathize with him. I believe that somewhere deep down, he would not hurt me or anyone at all.

I later began to wish I had known these things and dealt with them appropriately. Right now, they are ruining my entire life.

As said before, the red flags began to pop up too frequently, and most of them made me start to question my marriage to him. My fairy tale belief was crumbling.

I had never seen one who could lie and make it seem like it was the truth and nothing but the truth. Damn! It was shocking. That was the second red flag that popped its ugly head. It made me question if I was married to the person I thought I was, but each time I make such an evaluation, he would make me question my intentions in assuming such things about him.

For example, I suspected his attraction for teenage girls; but of course, he denied that fact. I felt terrible; I assumed such a thing about him and was very ashamed of myself. I then promised him not to think about such things again; besides, I loved him, and he was my soul mate, as he said. I felt he had changed.

 Within a short while, I felt like the princess I was again. He showed me off. It made people want to know our love story, and before you know, I became a teller of tales, but as expected, I did not tell EVERYTHING – the bad times, the cause of our disagreements, the shocking and unpredictable moments, and the flags and all.

One thing about my "prince charming" was he was very magnetic as well as charming, as his name tag implies.

Remember, in the beginning, I was the sole target, yeah? It turned out that I was not the only one, as I thought I was.

Well, it was years later when I realized that. He began sharing his charm with any attractive woman he meets, his sexuality and goodness, leaving little for me except I had something he needed. I subconsciously subjected myself to being an audience for his one-man show.

Going out with him was another thing entirely. I was never allowed to mingle but to glue myself to his side as he wows the room, capturing everyone's attention. It made me believe that everyone loved him. He gave his attention to any woman, no matter the age or marital status. He would make them laugh, giggle, or smile; things I had been unable to do because he had sucked every form of positive emotion from me.

I found myself emotionally exhausted in my marriage. I could not focus on anything except trying to get through my day with no hassle. Everything was blamed on me. He accused me, I blamed myself; and then I blamed it on my lovely kids. I could not even handle my kids. He never agreed to my input, my decisions, my advice, nothing. He compared me with every female he had met. He made me downcast every passing day. He never helped with raising the kids either.

One day, I wanted to get the groceries from the store after seeing the dentist, and I told him to assist with the kids ensuring they get to school early. He said I should figure everything out like every other mother. Why would he say that? Did he marry the other mothers or me? Well, I had to multitask, and before the day was over, I was fagged out.

Every day, I say to myself, "If only I knew what I was getting into," but it was too late to cry.

As if these things were not enough, the abuses began.

The few years of my life in that marriage were hell for me. Most times, I would stay indoors because I would not want people to see my already-ruined face. Now, he never hit me, but I had bruises and scars and the blue rings around my eyes, which were gotten from crying. Most times, he would pin me down, squeezing my neck, threatening to kill me, and at the same time, telling me how much he loves me. If I could call him anything, I would call him a psychopath. Well, he did not succeed in killing me but in making me dizzy and out of breath. After all these, he would then break down and cry, promising he would never actually hurt me. During all these "rituals," I would not utter a word or try to fight back because the last time I did, I "almost" died. It was entirely useless. I would stay put and listen to his whining, telling me of all the trouble I was and how he is the only man who can put up with my "shit."

After ten years of being emotionally destroyed to the point of almost losing my sanity and questioning my existence, I consoled myself with the fact that I was indeed lucky to have him. I could not trust myself anymore. I felt crazy because when I bring up things that he did in the past, he would always have a counter-answer to them, and it made me worry and also made me believe that I was indeed crazy.

Apart from being physically abused, I was mentally abused. In what way, you may ask. I was convinced that my mental health is not in any way healthy. I was confident that my understanding was false in almost every way. I social life was stopped. I could not even visit my parents or my friends. If I decide to go anywhere, once I am back, I am always "interrogated" like I committed a crime and thought I would get away with it. The annoying part is that when I say the truth, it becomes a lie to him. Unnecessary questions would be asked, like, "why did I spend so much time there, what was I talking about, did I give my phone number to any guy, did I have sex while I was there, did I think of cheating on him, why would I lie to him, why is my hair shabby, why did I change clothes, etc.". I then began to ask myself if I did those things without knowing. It sucked, honestly.

As my fairy tale faded before my eyes, I became a neglected wife. I was ignored. The kids bless their souls did not look at me like a bad mother, but they could not help my situation. I cried all the time. He gave me no attention. He was all about himself. He never got me anything. I got my clothes the little way I could. I was even told to quit my job because he believed I was flirting with every guy at work and also having sex with them. No trust! I could not feel his presence in my life or the house. He was like the wind; always gone in seconds.

The silent treatment, I got every dose of it. I decided to put myself in an emotional come to avoid having any form of feeling. It was my only way of survival. I was physically, mentally, and emotionally sick. I could not deal with the other red flags that were popping up. I did not have the strength for them. He began hiding money, travelling without informing me, coming back when he feels like partying and buying liquor for his underage friends, and other unspoken things.

One fateful day, I found myself again. I went online to find out how to deal with the situation I was in, and I was referred to a psychologist who was an expert on Narcissistic Personality Disorder. I became my knight in gleaming armor. I loved myself; I saved myself. I was no longer a victim. I set my life straight. I began to understand and educate myself. The first thing I did after all this realization was forgiving myself. I realized I was not the problem and decided to groom myself emotionally in rider to escape from the situation.

I found freedom and peace. I gave myself enough space and time to heal. Looking back now, I began to recognize the woman I was meant to be. I had grown from being a scared, fragile being to a brave, strong, and resilient woman, with lots of love to give herself and the world.

The one thing I realized I was not was CRAZY. I was sane. I was whole.

Chapter 4: Defining a Narcissist and Narcissism

We all have people in our lives that are incredibly confident and think highly of themselves. But, while they might not be the most pleasant sort to have around, these people are at best egocentric, if they do manage to have a relatively normal life. Narcissists, on the other hand, have many problems in multiple areas of their life, such as work, relationships, and finances. So, what's the difference between a self-centered person and a narcissist? Why can one have a normal life while the other struggles?

Now let's further focus on the traits of a narcissist, to understand the magnitude of this personality disorder fully, we'll see how it stands out from other well-known personality disorders such as psychopathy and sociopathy.

What Are The Traits Of A Narcissist?

An Exaggerated Sense of Self-Importance

The self-importance that a narcissist experience is different from vanity or extreme confidence. It's best described as "grandiosity," which defines a sense of superiority built on unrealistic terms. Narcissists believe that they are unique and seek to associate themselves with people/places/situations of high status, as they perceive themselves as being too good for ordinary or average things. This sense of being better than others is often built inside their mind and not based on real-life achievements. They will expect others to treat them as if they are superior, and to do that; they will resort to lying about their abilities, achievements, and always paint themselves as being the better person in any situation, be it relationships or work-related.

In short, a narcissist plays the part of the superior one, in all aspects of life, and will resort to anything to maintain this status, including lying, twisting and diminishing others.

The Constant Need for Attention and Validation

While they do foster that sense of superiority, they are somewhat aware of the illusory aspect of it. This is why they need constant praise and recognition to keep the illusion alive. For a narcissist, compliments are not enough. They will seek people that will offer them constant validation, and that will cater to their needs at all times, without ever giving anything back. They expect the people around them to put them on a pedestal, and even the slightest of critiques will be taken as a personal attack and will result in the narcissist becoming abusive.

A relationship with a narcissist can only be one-sided. They are too self-absorbed and cannot put themselves in their partner's shoes and understand their feelings and emotions.

Entitlement

Despite them not being deserving of any special treatment, a narcissist will feel abnormally entitled to the finer things in life. They will expect people to act in a certain way and always be at their disposal. Anyone that does not comply with that will be met with some form of aggression, going as far as being cut from the narcissist's life. They believe that they deserve everything they wish for, and they are not afraid to show it.

Exploiting The People in Their Life

As we touched on briefly at the start of this chapter, narcissists are incapable of feeling empathy, almost like an empty vessel. For a narcissist, the people in their lives are only a means to an end, more like tools and objects than actual human beings. They do anything to satisfy their own needs, and they will resort to exploiting the people in their life, without feeling any remorse, guilt, or shame for it. This is why it is extremely dangerous to have a narcissist in your life. It is hard to truly understand how someone is incapable of feeling empathy, remorse, or guilt as these are all emotions most people experience, and we automatically assume all humans have.

Narcissists have no problem with exploiting anyone, in any situation, as long as they get what they want, and they will never take responsibility for hurting others. They will keep 'stonewalling' (avoiding answering questions, take responsibility for their actions as if you are speaking to a wall) you until you are confused and docile. All the relationships they build are based on their needs. They will often ensure that they have multiple people to cater to their needs, be it shelter, money, sex, or other sorts of favors.

Living in an Imaginary World

A narcissist has a very frail relationship with reality. He or she prefers to live in their own fantasy world in which they can paint whatever image of themselves they want, pushing aside any details that don't work in their favor. They are willingly lying to themselves to protect the feeling of superiority that's detrimental to their survival, and annihilating contradictions or facts that go against their warped logic. Because they are insecure deep inside, this fantasy world works as their means of facing an unsatisfying reality. It allows them to feed their superiority with illusions of success, fame, popularity, and whatever they might need, and their defensive systems react heavily whenever something threatens or tries to reveal the illusion.

Putting Others Down to Lift Themselves Up

The inner core of the narcissist is threatened by anyone that has something they lack, be it money, success, or simply the admiration of others. They will do anything to diminish a person that threatens their self-importance, by acting condescending, using insults, bullying, and any other means available to 'scoop out' someone's self-worth. No matter how much they end up hurting people, narcissists only care about keeping their own fantasies alive, and will never feel remorseful or take responsibility for their actions.

Monopolizing

A conversation with a narcissist is pretty much like watching TV. They like to be the center of attention, and they will do whatever they can to have the last word, even if that means cutting others short or acting as if others have nothing valuable to say. Everything must revolve around them, no matter what, and they will display strong feelings of envy whenever they are not the focal point of a situation.

With a narcissist, everything is one-sided: relationships, conversations, situations. Simply because they are solely interested in themselves, and anything else only matters if they can use it to their own benefit.

Unstable MOOD

Whenever they find themselves slipping from their fantasy and face how far from the perfect persona they actually are, a narcissist will display a wide range of emotions. They will feel vulnerable, sad, and might even experience episodes of depression. Also, because of their weak ability to cope with reality, they have a tough time adapting to change or new situations, and they handle stress poorly. In the last effort to protect themselves, narcissists will lash out to the people around them, abusing them to regain that sense of superiority and control that they need. They won't back down from anything if it means that their illusion is kept alive. This fragility combined with their lack of empathy, remorse, and guilt makes the narcissist a toxic, abusive factor in any relationship, no matter how hard the other person may try to please them.

There is a great deal of confusion regarding three well-known types of personality disorders, that being narcissism, psychopathy, and sociopathy. What sets them apart from each other? How do we know what we are dealing with?

Both psychopathy and sociopathy are considered special types of personality disorders called antisocial personality disorders. They share multiple traits such as deceitfulness, aggression, irritability, a tendency towards committing criminal acts, lack of remorse or empathy in general, and not being able to take responsibility for their actions.

What sets them apart from the very beginning is that psychopaths are born while sociopaths are made. What does that mean? It is widely agreed that, although environmental factors, traumas, and different types of abuse influence both disorders, psychopathy is the main result of a faulty development in the parts of the brain that deal with emotions and impulse control. Psychopaths lack emotions and an ability to comprehend emotional responses from early infancy while sociopaths are results of trauma, and they can develop this disorder in any stage of their life. The rates of sociopathy are quite high. Statistically, 1 in 25 US citizens is a sociopath, which is very grim.

Narcissists share some traits with these antisocial disorders such as the lack of empathy and their inflated sense of self, but they are usually not aggressive in a physical way, and they are not impulsive. A narcissist's aggression comes from their verbal abuse and manipulation and is rarely physical. Their need to be admired by others, and thus their dependence on other people's attention also sets them apart from the field of antisocial personality disorders. Out of the two, we could say that narcissism most resembles sociopathy, seeing as it is a disorder that comes as a result of multiple factors and is not caused by undeveloped brain functions. It's only the narcissist's desire to achieve "perfection" that makes him less likely to commit criminal acts, that distinctively sets them apart from the destructive sociopath.

Knowing what a narcissist is, and what it's not, is crucial if you want to understand the sort of person that you have or had next to you, and how to successfully break free from them. Don't forget that, their lack of empathy makes it impossible to have a healthy relationship with them, so it's not your fault that it didn't work out. You deserve to be happy and loved, as much as anyone else in this world, so never feel guilty about leaving a narcissist behind.

What Causes Narcissism?

When looking at the statistics, the figure of approximately one percent of the population having narcissistic personality disorder seems eerily high—uncomfortably high, perhaps. By now, we've built up a broader and stronger idea of who is normally affected by it. As we can see, narcissistic personality disorder certainly doesn't discriminate, though there is a number of criteria that make somebody more likely to have the disorder, and it does seem to occur more commonly in men than in women.

Despite looking at the people that narcissistic personality disorder occurs within—or, rather, the groups which seem to present with his disorder the most—we still haven't looked at a huge number of the root causes. The prime focus of this chapter is going to be looking at the different causes of narcissistic personality disorder and what can actually lead to somebody developing this horrible disorder.

The exact causes of narcissistic personality disorder are currently unknown. There are a number of indirect suppositions as to what causes it, and all of these culminate into what is the general modern vision of what leads to the development of this disorder.

The going consensus on what leads to the development of narcissistic personality disorder is that it's ultimately a combination of genetic, social, environmental, and biological factors. The exact role that each of these plays in the development of this disorder can vary depending upon the individual and the exact subtype of the disorder developed can vary equally as much. That is to say, there is no sure cocktail of causes that will lead to the development of one specific subtype or another.

In order to dive into the big question of "why does this happen?" a bit more, we're going to be looking at this one-by-one in order to come to a firmer understanding on what causes narcissistic personality disorder.

Firstly, let's look at the genetic aspect: there is a lot of evidence that the disorder itself can be inherited. The existence of a family member with the disorder makes it far more likely that a given individual will develop the disorder themselves. Studies performed on twins have been rather conducive to showing that there is an inheritable aspect to the disorder.

It can be difficult, though, to determine how much of this is because of the person growing up with somebody who has the disorder—for example, if somebody's father were to have narcissistic personality disorder. This no doubt would lead to the child taking in that influence and being, to one extent or another, impacted by the disorder and more likely to develop it themselves. In this case, narcissistic personality disorder could be seen as both a genetic and a social disorder.

Beyond the genetic factors, there are a number of different environmental factors at play as well. Here, we're going to be looking at both the social and environmental catalysts to the development of narcissistic personality disorder. These are largely thought to play the biggest part in the development of the disorder—larger than either the genetic or biological causes, though with environment and biology likely playing equal parts or with environment only slightly weighted in favor compared to biology.

One of the largest catalysts for the development of narcissistic personality disorder is when a child learns manipulative behavior from either their parents or their friends. Manipulative parents are extremely common, and unfortunately, manipulative parenting styles weren't condemned for a rather long time. With developmental psychology and emotional abuse only becoming topics that were largely discussed in the second half of the 20th century, what results is the fact that there are still some rather ancient parenting styles that are incredibly unhealthy. More than that, it doesn't just come down to the parenting style; it also comes down to a person's general way of life. It's unfortunate, but due to the way that manipulative behavior works, it's possible for a manipulative person to surround themselves with people they can manipulate and never have to change their behavior. Because of this, they could teach this to a child as the norm.

With attitudes on parenting largely shifting in the twenty-first century, this problem will hopefully become less and less prominent as people start to discuss things such as mental and emotional abuse more and they become more acceptable topics of discourse. Until then, this will remain a rather prominent catalyst.

This goes hand-in-hand with another catalyst for the development of narcissistic personality disorder: emotional abuse in childhood. Manipulative behavior and emotional abuse aren't necessarily one and the same, but they do often go hand-in-hand. In the latter case, one may develop narcissistic personality disorder as a defense mechanism or coping mechanism. These can be some of the hardest cases to deal with from a psychological perspective because dealing with them means dealing with a much deeper trauma. This is compared to just trying to make people rationalize their position in other individuals who didn't have to endure emotional abuse as a child.

That isn't to say, though, that a narcissist may necessarily have developed this as a defense or coping mechanism. In fact, many people develop the disorder as a result of things which happen to them in other ways. For example, a lot of people like to take the post that there's no such thing as excessive praise for a child. However, when a child is developing, many of the actions which occur to them—if they stick out in any way—will be intensely formative and cemented into their brain forever unless they make a very active attempt to unlearn them.

If somebody is excessively praised, they may develop the idea that they're unable to do any wrong. This happens often with single parents who don't wish to lose the respect or adoration of their child, unfortunately, and I've seen it pop up in quite a few cases of such. Likewise, if a child is excessively criticized, they may develop narcissistic personality disorder as a defense mechanism.

If people tell somebody all the time that they're exceptionally beautiful or talented with little basis in reality or little realistic, earthbound feedback in response to the praise, they're at risk for the development of narcissistic personality disorder. If people overvalue somebody or indulge them too often, that person becomes far more likely to develop the disorder.

In essence, the mind desires some sort of equilibrium in terms of its interactions with other people. It does whatever it can to reach out for this equilibrium and seek it out. Believe it or not, not all minds are equally resilient and able to so handily endure some of the stresses or excesses of life. In other words, a lot of what causes narcissistic personality disorder can be seen as over-parenting. Someone who excessively gives praise, criticism, or manipulates their child puts their child at risk for the development of narcissistic personality disorder.

Parents who are narcissists themselves will often use their children as a means of self-validation and force their narcissistic behaviors onto their children. This lead, generally, to either resentment or the development of Stockholm syndrome. In the former case, people may drop contact with their parents or limit contact as much as possible. In the latter, they will often model themselves after their parents.

In terms of biological factors which correspond to the development of this disorder, there isn't a whole lot of research to work with. As I said earlier, finding finite study opportunities for narcissistic personality disorder can be difficult. However, what studies have been done have shown that the areas of the brain having to do with empathy, emotion, and compassion generally are not nearly as large as they are in neurotypical people or people without mental disorders.

One question many people might ask while reading this is whether or not they can tell if their child is a narcissist. If you picked this book up in the first place because you're worried that your child may have this disorder, then I've got a relatively disappointing answer for you: your guess is as good as mine.

Chapter 5: Signs You Are Dating a Narcissist

Dating a narcissist isn't a child's play and not a thing to be attempted by the ignorant or faint-hearted. However, your greatest weapon in this journey is knowledge – knowledge of yourself and your potential narcissistic lover. According to George Bernard Shaw, knowledge creates or inspires courage. Yes, only the courageous can date a narcissist and stay or come out of the relationship unscathed, mentally and emotionally. Lack of knowledge, according to Shaw, creates fear. Therefore, seek knowledge, which Shaw says, will create courage.

Note that narcissists are skillful at hiding their true colors. As a result, you need to be aware of how the mind of a narcissist works for you to identify one. In fact, people with narcissistic personality can be recognized because of the following characteristics, as all they do will revolve around this.

- Entitlement: They believe in getting what they want.
- One-mindedness: To a narcissist, only a single point of view exists—theirs.
- Absence of empathy: They cannot understand how others feel due to their low emotional quotient.
- No sense of proportion: All you need to set a narcissist off is a slight mistake, and you see them making a mountain out of a molehill.

There are many signs that will reveal you are in a relationship with a narcissist. The four characteristics discussed above are usually the underlying cause. Here are the signs you will see when dating one:

They Often Threaten You

Watch out for threats from your partner. It might be a threat to leave you, to blackmail you, etc. It is usually common with a narcissist. Watch out for statements like:

- "If you do not do this by _____, consider this relationship over."
- "Everyone will know what kind of person you are."
- "I am better off without you, go ahead and leave."

Excessive Need for Attention and Validation

If your partner has a high need for validation, there is a tendency you are dealing with a narcissist. They will try every means to get your attention. To a narcissist, external validation is important for them to feel good and wanted.

The sad part, however, is that it does not count much. Even though they so crave validation and approval from you, it is never enough. No matter how much you let them know you care for them and approve of them, it doesn't soothe them. This is due to the fact that they do not see anyone truly loving them. This can be traced to the root of a narcissist because despite being self-absorbed, they are insecure deep-down—hence the desire for more and more approval.

A Huge Need for Control

A narcissist is never contented with life. This makes him try all in his capacity to mold things to his liking. As a result of this, they have a compulsion for control. Their sense of entitlement also makes it logical for them to want to be in control.

A narcissist has an idealized way in which people should act. When people fail to behave as expected, it upsets them. Since you've already deviated, they are clueless about what to expect next, which throws them off-balance.

The narcissist wants you to act and do as they please so they can reach their idealized conclusion. To them, you are just a pawn to achieve their selfish desire—a robot that should be controlled and told what to do!

Inability to Accept Responsibility

While narcissists strive to be in control, they also have the tendency to dodge responsibility for the outcome. This only changes if the result goes as expected; otherwise, they feel inadequate and place all the blame on you. Accepting fault is never in their nature as they just have to deflect.

There are times the blame could be generalized—the government, the law enforcement agent, the caregivers, etc. Other times, a particular person could be the object of his blame, like his parents, his colleague, his boss, etc. Most times, however, the blame falls on the person most emotionally close to the narcissist.

They cannot do without blaming, as it helps keep up with their idealized sense of perfection.

Perfectionism

In the narcissist's world, they are perfect. As a result, they expect you and everyone else to be perfect. Narcissists have this invisible script well planned out in their head, dictating how things should go. Events, life, and people around them must follow this carefully crafted script, just like they want it.

This, without a doubt, is an impossible demand, which eventually makes the narcissist miserable and dissatisfied.

Emotional Reasoning

You might be frustrated about the behavior of your partner. You tried everything in your effort to explain to him and make him see how much pain and suffering he is causing you. You expect him will adjust if he understands how much he hurts you. But since a narcissist is only caught up in his world, your explanations make little to no sense to him. Even if he admits he understands, he really does not.

Thus to a narcissist, their actions and decisions are usually based on how they feel. The only reason they need to get the latest Lamborghini is how driving it makes them feel. They are not bothered by the fact that it is a burden on the family and budget. At the slightest provocation and discomfort, a narcissist could quit his job with the hope of moving to another one or starting a business. To a narcissist, their problem can only be solved by something or someone else, not themselves.

Fear and Anxiety

The life of a narcissist revolves around fear, yet for most of them, this fear is deeply buried. They fear being wrong, being seen as incapable, not being accepted, etc. They fear being fired, being tested, being considered inadequate. It is because of this fear that a narcissist hardly trusts anyone.

The deeper your relationship gets, the more he becomes suspicious of you. Narcissists have a phobia for true intimacy as it makes them vulnerable, which could expose their weak points. All your assurance and reassurance makes no difference, as their imperfection is a personal turnoff.

An Inability to be Vulnerable

Since a narcissist cannot truly process feelings, and since they always need to protect their image, it is difficult for them to truly connect with others. Since they are full of themselves and their ways, they cannot consider things from another person's perspective. Emotionally, they are lonely, which makes them needy.

When a relationship does not give them what they want, they pull the plug as soon as possible and jump to the next one. Wired deep in their DNA is the need to always make everything as they want it, have someone feel their pain and sympathize with them. On the contrary, however, they are not capable of responding to someone else's need.

Relationships of all kinds with narcissists follow three stages: Love bombing, devaluing, and discarding. This predictable cycle is followed regardless of the type of relationship is forged with the narcissist; narcissists will repeat this with romantic partners, children, friends, and anyone else in their lives who accept it. Those who do not accept it are either demeaned and attacked or completely disregarded and dismissed. While the three stages are followed, narcissists' behavior changes somewhat depending on the kind of relationship and what is socially acceptable within those relationship's norms.

Signs You Are in a Relationship with a Narcissist

A romantic relationship with a narcissist begins perfectly. It feels like it is out of a storybook about true love, and for a good reason; both the storybook and the narcissist's persona are fictitious. The narcissist works hard to draw in his target, seeking to make the target fall hard and fast for the narcissist. This is accomplished through mirroring and love-bombing.

The narcissistic romantic partner may send flowers and love notes to work every day while constantly texting their target about how beautiful they are and how perfect the two of them are together. The romantic partner may invite their target on dates constantly and will push for the relationship to move at a much quicker pace than is typical, even if the target is uncomfortable with it. The narcissist will be more controlling than the target likes, but the target will justify this as being overly-protective or due to past trauma.

Over time, as the target becomes more attached to the narcissist, the narcissist's mask begins to crumble. First it may crack slightly, but eventually, it disintegrates, leaving the narcissist in all his glory, unmasked and unbearable while you find yourself too in love with the mask to leave its pieces on the floor without trying to salvage it. With the victim firmly attached to the narcissist, the narcissist finds he free to be himself. If he feels slighted in any way, he may lash out at the target, saying things that are hurtful or demeaning, or even yelling and intimidating the target into submission.

When in a narcissistic relationship, it is common to feel lonely, or as if you are unimportant, as the narcissist stops putting your desires first as soon as he feels you are firmly within his grasp. He no longer has to go through the effort of winning you over because you have already found yourself head-over-heels in love thanks to the intensely wonderful honeymoon period. He may move on to other tactics to keep you around, such as demeaning you or gas lighting you. You will be left with self-esteem as wounded as the narcissist's, but unlike the narcissist, yours can heal back into something healthy if given the self-care you need.

At the end of the relationship, the narcissist discards you; he may have moved onto a new source to feed his narcissistic supply, or he may have decided that the effort in maintaining you as useful is no longer worthwhile.

Is There a Future for a Relationship Touched by Narcissism?

We have covered a lot of information about the victim's future but what about the narcissist's future.

It isn't a nice picture if the narcissist won't get help. If they don't, it will be likely that they will just jump from one relationship to the next. If they do find a long-term relationship, their partner won't be really fulfilled and happy. They will more than likely just be putting up with the narcissist.

If during the duration of the narcissist's relationship they had children, the bad news is their children will probably develop narcissist behaviors since they were exposed to it through their growing years. Even though there isn't a definite answer to what causes narcissism, there are suggestions that experiences during childhood has firm links toward developing the disorder during their adolescent or adult years.

Narcissists are known to become bitter with time. This is mainly due to people coming into their lives and then leaving them and they can't figure out why. They will always put the blame onto someone else and will never see they had a role in them leaving. Most narcissistic traits get worse with age as they experience more things through their life.

You can see it is a very bleak picture and this is the sad truth about the narcissist's life. People will only stay around if they are treated nice. If they get treated like crap, they will eventually leave. Some might not get to that point but relationships with narcissists are usually empty and don't have respect and true love.

The biggest price any narcissist will pay for their actions with time will be loneliness and not ever knowing what a meaningful relationship really is. The deepest and most meaningful relationship a narcissist will have will be with them.

Should We Blame Social Elements?

You almost know all there is to know about narcissists and the issues and traits that go with it. We also need to look at another area. Are social elements to blame for the increasing number of narcissists?

True narcissists are very rate but it is a term that we hear more and more. For this reason, narcissistic behaviors are more common now, so we need to find out why? Is it all the social pressures we have to deal with? Is it social media? Is it because we are pressured to own the best, look, the best, and be the best?

It is unfair to put the blame of narcissism at modern society's feet. It does make one wonder if it did have a hand in it. Social media makes us aware of the way other people live and look. The influences of social media tell us that if we want to be the best, we must look our best, and this means we have to use a certain product. We get bombarded with people constantly taking selfies and full body photos and then using filters and Photoshop to change their appearance drastically. The majority of what we see just isn't real. Now, do you wonder why we have all these unrealistic expectations of what we should look like, what we should be, and what we need to aim for?

No one is completely sure what causes narcissism, so it is the things we are exposed to in life? Most of the narcissistic cases are thought to come from things we experienced during childhood, but what caused those experiences? What makes someone act a specific way? What makes someone create trauma to another human that can cause them to develop a certain personality disorder? It is hard to figure out, but you have to take into account all the possibilities.

We might not completely understand what causes narcissism, and there is a specific amount of stigma attached to it. If we try to be the best, it will be a constant, fruitless task. We should try to just be ourselves.

When talking about future generations, it is our responsibility to make sure our children are brought up to be happy just being who they are, without have to constantly compete to reach unrealistic goals. If we can do this, we are going to raise a generation of young people who are fulfilled, respectful, and well-mannered. These are great boosts toward avoiding trauma and personality disorders.

Chapter 6: Narcissistic Abuse

Narcissists don't love each other. They're actually driven by guilt. It is the idealized image of themselves that they are persuaded to embody, to admire. But narcissists feel deep down the gap between their façade and their shameful self. We work hard to avoid this embarrassment. That difference extends to other codependents, but a narcissist uses defense mechanisms that disrupt relationships and cause pain and harm to his self-esteem. Most of the coping mechanisms of the narcissist are coercive— that is why the word ' narcissistic violence' is used. Furthermore, someone can be violent, but not a narcissist. Those with other mental illnesses, such as bi-polar disorganization and antisocial personality disorder (sociopathy), borderline personality disorders, and many codependents without a mental illness, are also violent. Abuse is abuse, regardless of the diagnosis of the abuser. When you are victimized, the main challenges are: recognizing it clearly, developing a support system, and learning to improve and defend yourself.

Abuse of Narcissism can be mental, physical, financial, spiritual, or sexual. Several examples of abuses you may not have heard include verbal abuse: intimidation, bullying, accusing, insulting, demanding, ordering, intimidating, ridicule, sarcasm, screaming, opposing, criticizing, interrupting, blocking, and calling names. Remember that many people make requests, use sarcasm, interrupt, object, condemn, accuse, or block you from time to time. Take into account the meaning, intent, and degree of behavior before calling it narcissistic violence.

Manipulation: Manipulation usually influences someone indirectly in a way that fosters the manipulator's objectives. It sometimes demonstrates secret hostility. On the surface, words seem harmless— even complimentary–but below, you feel disgusted or feel a hostile intention. You may not know it as such if you have encountered deception as a result.

Emotional chantage: Threats, frustration, threats, coercion, or retribution may include emotional chantage. It is a form of manipulation that causes you doubts. You feel fear, guilt, and culpability, also called "FOG," which makes you doubt your perception of reality intentionally, and you believe you are mentally incompetent.

Rivalry: rivalry and the desire to be on top always, sometimes by ethical means. Cheating in a game, for example.

Negative contrast: Contrast to you with the narcissist or other people is needless.

Sabotage: Disruptive interference with your vengeance or financial gain actions or relationships.

Use and object: using and take advantage of yourself for your personal purposes regardless of your feelings or needs.

Lying: Persistent failure to avoid liability and achieve the goals of the narcissist.

Withholding: retaining from your things like money, gender, contact, or affection.

Disclaimer: Ignoring the wishes of a child the perpetrator is responsible for. Requires endangerment of infants, i.e., having or leaving children in dangerous circumstances.

Invasion of privacy: Avoid your boundary by looking through your things, by phone, by e-mail; reject or pursue you; avoid confidentiality that you requested.

Attacking or slandering of character: spreading false rumors or lies to other people.

Violence: It involves blocking the expression, hair pulling, stuff throwing, and damage.

Financial abuse: Financial abuse may include manipulating you by means of economic domination, bribery, robbery, manipulation, or gambling, or by adding debt to you or selling your personal property.

Isolation: isolating yourself from your friends, family, or outside services by controlling, manipulating, verbally abusing, murdering characters, or any other method of abuse.

There is a spectrum of narcissism and the extent of violence. It can range from ignoring your feelings to violent attacks. Normally, narcissists do not take responsibility or blame you or others for their actions, but Others do and can experience guilt and self-reflection.

A more arrogant individual who acts maliciously, hostilely
It is regarded to always have "malignant narcissism. These are not troubled by remorse. You can be sadistic and enjoy inflicting pain. They can be so aggressive and unpronounced that they are antisocial. Paranoia places them in self-protection defensive-attack mode.

Malignant narcissism can look like sociopathy. Sociopaths have brains that have been malformed or impaired. We exhibit narcissistic tendencies, but not every narcissist is sociopathic. Their motives vary. Although narcissists promote an ideal person to be respected, sociopaths alter who they are in order to achieve their autonomous agenda. We should win at all costs and do not think about social norms or rules being violated. I don't like narcissists to bind to men. Narcissists don't want to be killed. They depend on the approval of others, but sociopaths can easily move away from relationships that don't serve them. While some narcissists often scheme to meet their goals, usually, they are more reactive than sociopaths who measure their intentions coldly.

Get help if you are with a narcissist, it is important to get support from outside to understand what is happening, to restore your self-esteem and trust, and to learn to communicate and to set borders effectively

Where most people believe regarding abuse-be, it spousal, parental, and so on-they tend to focus on physical abuse. However, the lasting Any abuse could have devastating effects. Mental and emotional abuse can be more harmful, especially if the perpetrator is close to the abused.

Perhaps the worst kind of abuse comes from the hands of those who are so busy that they do not see or think about the results of their actions. This kind of narcissistic abuse can be found in many different types of relationships, including parent, spouse, and even friendships. Emotional abuse by a narcissistic parent can be particularly insidious as it can impair the child's ability in the future to establish stable relationships. It was proposed that those suffering from emotional abuse as children tend to end up in similar abusive relationships as adults due to lack of an appropriate model of a healthy relationship.

In the US, the 1980s were seen as a time when self-centeredness and self-centeredness were not only appropriate; they were anticipated. The "Me Generation" created new narcissistic extremes. Many were willing to disregard for themselves the well-being of others.

Given this inner emphasis, most of the individuals we find were not true narcissists in the strictest sense when we think of this time. It was taken from the Greek story of a Naissus, a hunter who was the son of the god of the river Cephis and the nymph Liriope. He had such charm that he could not be stripped from desire himself. The lord Nemesis led him into a pool where he saw his own reflection and fell into love, only that he died there considering his own equal characteristics.

Narcissism is described as "inordinate obsession with self; excessive self-love; vanity" or "erotic pleasure derived from an appreciation of one's own physical or mental qualities that is a normal condition at a childhood personality developmental level." In 1968, psychological literature was added to an extreme form as a definable diagnosis.

The American Psychiatric Association's present Diagnostic and Statistical Manual (DSM-V) describes Narcissistic Personality Disorder as the pervasive of a grandiosity pattern (in perception or behavior), the need for recognition and a lack of empathy, starting in the early age and present in a variety of contexts as shown in five(s):

1. Has a great sense of self-importance (for example, exaggerated performances and talents, without comparable accomplishments, is expected to be recognized as superior).

2. Is concerned with limitless illusions of achievement, energy, light, beauty, or affection.

3. Believes that he or she is "special" and unique and that he or she can only be understood by or associated with other high-ranking or special people (or institutions).

4. Excessive admiration is needed.

5. Has an irrational sense of entitlement, i.e., of especially favorable treatment or automatic compliance with its requirements.

6. Is interpersonally exploitative, i.e., using others to achieve its own goals.

7. Lack of empathy: is unwilling to recognize or consider other people's feelings and needs.

8. Is envious of others or feels others envy him or her.

9. Shows rude, haughty behaviors or behaviors.

In fact, to warrant a diagnosis of Narcissistic Personality Disorder, the following criteria must be fulfilled: A. Significant impairments in personality function occur by 1. Functional impairments (a or b):

 a. Identity: unnecessary reference to others for self-definition, self-esteem control, unrealistic self-assessments between extremes, or shifting between extremes; emotional regulation represents self-esteem fluctuations.

b. Self-management: goal-setting depends on other people's consent; personal standards are unreasonably high to find ourselves exceptional or to low on the basis of a sense of entitlement, sometimes ignorant of one's own motives.

2 AND. Interpersonal impairments (a or b):

a. Empathy: the diminished capacity to understand or consider other people's feelings and needs; overly sensitive to other people's reactions only where considered to be self-relevant; over-or underestimated self-reaction on others.

b. Intimacy: relations largely superficial and occur in order to regulate self-esteem; mutuality constrained by little genuine interest in other interactions and by the need for personal gain Pathological personality characteristics in the following domain: 1. Intimacy: Characterized by antagonism:

a. Grandiosity: feelings of superiority, visible or covert; self-centeredness; a firm belief that you are better than others; a condescension to others.

b. Looking for attention: excessive attempts to attract and focus attention, searching for admiration.

c. The impairments in personality functioning and personality classification of the patient are fairly stable over time and consistent through circumstances.

d. Impairment of personality functioning and the signature speech of the individual are not better understood as a norm for the developmental or socio-cultural stage of each individual.

e. The change of temperament and characteristic speech of the patient is not only due to specific physiological effects (e.g., drug abuse, medicine) or a general medical disorder (e.g., serious head trauma).

While all this might seem daunting, we can see how a relationship with someone with Narcissistic Disorder could easily be turned into a living hell by concentrating on a few important parts of the diagnosis. As stated in the first quote, narcissistic people have decreased to be more important than others. We don't just sit on a pedestal, and we think others do the same thing. There is no healthy relationship between one person and the other, but narcissists are incapable of forming healthy relationships.

As can be seen in the second quote, there is a lack of empathy for others or a failure to shape intimate relations. The fact that "relationships [are] largely superficial and exist to control self-esteem" is particularly revealing (accent added).

One approach is a friendship with someone with Narcissistic Disorder of Personality. The individual receives all his attention and emotional support from the narcissist. These interactions are marked by verbal and psychological abuse, discouragement, grievances, and physical abuse also. Narcissists claim they can't make any error, so any relationship problems and even daily life problems are the responsibility of the other person. If an error is made, somehow, the partner is to blame.

The need for recognition and validation lead the narcissists to look for those who improve their inflated self-worth continuously. It represents a number of short partnerships and a long line of discarded partners. If the narcissist is engaged, he or she is likely to be unfaithful. Of course, the offender is blamed for not being attractive enough, loving enough, etc. If the infidelity is revealed, the victims of a narcissistic abuser are often shown to have similar features. The most common is a weak sense of self-worth, frequently followed by the inability to think for themselves. You spend years complaining that you are not good enough, not smart enough, not enough. Throughout time, these derogatory comments have been internalized. We question their own expertise. This encourages them to rely more on the narcissistic abuser and to build a co-dependency cycle.

This is one of the worst examples of narcissistic abuse of parental care. If the kids are constantly undermined, they grow up and believe they can't. Once they finally leave their abusive parents under control, they do not have the requisite coping skills to survive on their own. They doubt their own decision-making capabilities and are paralyzed by poor self-esteem; they work towards somebody who accepts and decides for them, despite their perceived defects. In short, they are linked to narcissistic abusers. We just abandon their family to end up with someone like the same people who first abused them.

Those with a narcissist can have a number of emotional and physical symptoms that are hard to attribute to the relationship because of the stress they face each day. It causes doubt, dissociation, bad food and sleep habits, and even symptoms of PTSD.

For those with a narcissist, it is particularly difficult to get help since they are programmed to look in their abuser for most, if not all, decision-making practices. Your poor self-esteem makes it easy for you to ignore the idea that you deserve more. Obviously, nobody else would have them in their minds. They should be content with their marriage, although they are unhappy. This is a theme that the perpetrator will also perpetuate.

Although challenging, the process of narcissistic abuse can be avoided. The first step should be to accept that no one deserves the narcissist's constant humiliation and demands. As the picture of oneself is returned to a healthy level, decisions can be made easier without the input of the abuser. For example, this is an extremely difficult method that can be assisted by externals, including professionals.

An individual is capable of abusing or hurting another person when he or she is hurt or angry. The difference between a narcissist and any other individual is the guilt. When you control, judge, withhold or criticize others (loved ones or anyone in general), you tend to feel guilty at some point in time, often when your anger or frustration subside. In the case of a narcissist, they never feel guilty about their actions.

The abuse of a narcissist can be:

- Emotional
- Physical
- Financial
- Sexual
- Mental or/and
- **Spiritual**

Narcissistic abuse is often emotional, and it is difficult for most individuals to identify that they are being abused. Manipulation, emotional threats and psychological intimidation are used to exercise control over you, which ultimately results in mental torture. They are experts in verbal abuse and manipulation, and they know how to push you to a state where you begin to doubt your own sanity.

Who is a Narcissist?

These people usually appear fun to be with since they present themselves as compassionate and loving personalities. Everybody would want to be friends or surround themselves with such people, and there are times when the relationship could become romantic. Narcissists are often deemed as the ideal choices for partners. You will love hanging around with them, but do you think they can be good partners?

Do you have a friend or are you in a relationship with someone who only loves talking about himself or herself? Were you shocked when they first snapped at you for talking about your problems? Did the person make you feel like your pain or struggle is nothing compared to what they have been through or are going through? Did they intentionally change the topic when you were explaining something of utmost importance?

A listening disorder is one of the main things you will come across with a narcissist. When you rewind it all, you will realize that you were doing the listening most of the time. It is quite difficult to maintain friendship with such an individual, It is difficult to talk to someone who does not want to hear you out or is quick to dismiss anything you say. However, the narcissist is very charming in the beginning of a romantic relationship. They would make you feel so special to the point of idolizing you, they tell you things like you are better than all the people they had ever been with. Their motive is to draw you in, eventually the abuse would start.

Chapter 7: Empathy and Empath

Growing as an empath in a family can be tough. It sometimes can be frightening in cases where one is not aware of being an empath. There is a constant internal, emotional battle in empaths between what they feel and feeling what others are feeling. Empaths have to practice self-care in order to have a healthy emotional and mental state. It can be a bit frustrating when an empath can't place his or her finger on what is causing a shift in their moods. One has to be aware of the emotions they are picking up in order to find a way to balance it.

An empath has to master a way of resisting the urge to get wrapped up in what other people are feeling. Detaching from what other people are feeling is helpful not only to you but to people around you since you'll be at your best and most reasonable self at most times. This helps in being calm and being able to solve a problem without being consumed by it.

One can be a naturally born empath or might be triggered by something. In either case, having empathy involves having highly heightened levels of sensitivity. Here are the sources of empathy;

- Genetics

Having emotional or super sensitive parents can be transferred to the offspring. This makes it genetic.

- Trauma

Going through trauma can increase your sensitivity levels. In most cases, kids who went through emotional or even physical pain. Being raised by alcoholic parents or even parents that neglect them makes them feel unseen. This helps them have a high level of sensitivity to the outside world that usually doesn't care. This sharpens then to feel emotions around them since they developed a different defense mechanism to the world than a child who was raised by better parents.

- Supportive parenting

Being raised by parents who help you become self- aware and supportive in every way can be helpful in nurturing empathy in kids. These parents help children honor what they have understood it better. They can also be done through parents being a good example to the kids. Children copy what they see. Even in times when they aren't aware of it.

- Temperament

This is when a baby is born with high sensitivity. You can see it by hoe respond to things like light and temperature from the moment they are born.

Are You an Empath?

You might not figure it out yet. It is vital to be self- aware. It's the only way to live a better life as an empath. Here are some of the characteristics of an empath;

- People call you sensitive
- You occasionally need to recharge or keep to yourself after socializing with people.
- You do your best to help people to the extent of going out of your way to help.
- You go through high levels of emotions when in certain situations or environments.
- People think you are confident.

- Intimate relations overwhelm you.
- You prefer sleeping alone.

Being an empath can be a great thing. Most empaths help people without putting in much effect or need much convincing to do it. They tend to be more willing to be of help to other people.

Some of the benefits of being an empath while growing up are;

- Better relations with people. As mentioned earlier, empaths are great at communicating due to the fact that they already know what it feels like to be in someone else's shoes. They, most of the time, know what to say or respond.
- You are able to build trust easily. People are able to trust you since you are able to prove yourself during hard times.
- Conducive environment for problem-solving.
- Go-getter. Empaths don't need validation; they just go for it. They follow their intuition at all times and they are not afraid.

When it comes to relationships, empaths have a hard time. This is because they feel their partner's emotions as if they were their own. It's challenging because they feel them at a higher intensity. The idea of romantic relationships is a bit scary to an empath. Most relationship empaths have a hard time due to the fact that sometimes they don't even know what their fears are.

A relationship with an empath can only work when they know what their fears are together with their boundaries. At times they can't even set clear boundaries or even communicate their needs clearly.

Here is the thing with empathy; you have to recognize that you are one in order to handle it better. It's easy to get engulfed in other people's feelings and problems solving that an empath can forget about themselves. An empath needs to be self- aware to avoid losing himself or herself.

How do you know if you are a relationship empath? Ask yourself these questions from the book of The Power of Surrender by Judith Orloff, to find out;

- Are you labeled as a sensitive person?
- Does the idea of losing yourself to someone you are romantically involved with scare you?
- Do you feel drained by togetherness and need time alone?
- Do you prefer sleeping alone sometimes?
- Do you prefer to stay in the same room when you travel?
- Do you feel overwhelmed by noise, smell, crowds, or excessive talking?

If you have answered yes to at least three questions, then you belong to a unique group of the relationship empaths. Finding out if you are a relationship empath is the first step towards finding a life- long partner. You may notice that traditional expectations about relationships and marriage don't work for you. This is simply due to the fact that an empath needs space to recharge once they are exhausted.

Growing up in empath relationships can be difficult to manage yet essential in our lives. Here is how you can cope with relationships;

- Socializing time

Have a limited amount of socializing. Explain to your partner how important it is to you to limit the time you spend around social groups. Do this before you burn out. Have your won means of transport in case your partner prefers to stay a bit longer. It's all about finding common ground.

- Compatibility

How compatible is your partner? Do they understand your nature? Do they understand how important alone time is for you? The wrong person will crucify you for being overly sensitive.

- Quite time all through the day

Get in the habit of taking time off to decompress as much as you need all through the day. Take your time to take walks, breathe, and meditate.

- Sleeping divorce

Explain to your partner that you may need days off to sleep alone. This is why the traditional expectations of marriage or relationships don't work. You need some days alone. Empaths can get lonely at times, so agree what days or for how long you will be sleeping on different beds and different rooms as well.

- Square footage

Being together all the time is not good. Breathing space is a must. Discuss what space arrangement will work for you. You can different bedrooms or even bathrooms. Sometimes even hanging a sheet to separate you two when in the same room can help.

- Energy vibrations

Notice the energy around someone when they talk and how it affects you as an empath. Is it an effect you can handle? Do they match their energy? They say vibrations speak way louder than words at all times.

Take note of everything. This is to avoid getting involved with the wrong person. Note that protecting your energy and how you use it is of utmost importance.

One has to be creative to save one's relationship or even marriages. Empaths need a space that's safe for their emotions and energy. Once they feel safe enough in relationships and let go, boundaries need to be set. The worst that can happen for a relationship empath is losing themselves to their partner. However, the internal pull and push in emotions keep them from giving in to their partners.

Setting boundaries raises one question that can be frightening, what if I set boundaries and then no one wants to be in your life? People think of boundaries as these scary lines with huge letters of 'Do not Approach.' This is not the case. Boundaries are meant to protect you, to give you the space you need. It cultivates respect and clarity.

It allows you to keep your energy in check and understand your capacity on all levels.

How do you create your boundaries and uphold them at all times? With self- awareness, an intention setting boundaries is possible. A fine line of boundaries is saying yes or no when you mean it. It's like honoring your binderies. Without that, you end up being resentful or even disengaged with the people around you.

Understanding what boundaries represent is what will motivate people to enforce them and respect them. This is how you can do that;

- Boundaries are about being authentic and not scaring people away. Once the boundaries are set, you are clear with what line not to cross. This allows you to interact with people in the most authentic way possible.

- Boundaries don't mean you are unavailable. It's more of honoring your needs and your energy. You are your own protector of your energy. Boundaries help you with self- care and support needs.
- Boundaries are about self- respect and not self- importance. Having boundaries can make you come across as someone who exaggerates their self- importance. However, this is not the case. You set the boundaries due to self- respect. to allow yourself to grow and shine in your own way. They help one to maintain a safe zone for one's self.

Some of the clear boundaries an empath can set are;

- Leave if you need to

Sometimes we stay in situations hoping the other person will change. As an empath, this can take a hard toll on emotionally. It can be draining. If the person you are with puts you down more than lifting you up, it's time to leave. Mental abuse is as bad as physical abuse. Once one starts making you feel like it's wrong to be the way you are as a person, it's time to cut them off.

- Compromise

Do not compromise yourself at any time. Do what you are comfortable with. People around you will always remind you about how sensitive you are. You have to get used to that. That shouldn't be a reason to compromise yourself. There is always going to be a lot of emotions running through you. That's who an empath is. There is nothing that can be done to change that. if people around you don't understand that, then it's okay.

- Empaths are strong people

Absorbing what other people fell and still be able to be yourself is not an easy task. Growing up as an empath can be made easier by self-awareness. You need to know what energies you are picking and how to handle them. Take note of environments that make you strive as an individual and those that put you down. Most people will term growing up as am empath as a curse. It can be a burden hard to bear. Growing up as an empath comes with some myths or rather misunderstandings. Some of them are:

- Growing a thick skin

You will hear this a lot from people around you. You don't have to listen to them. What you can do is understand you better and know what works for you. Growing a thick skin is almost impossible. It's like trying to change who you are and that's not how it works.

- Mental illness

People assume empaths are mentally ill. That's not the case. They just have a burden they can't drop. They act as magnets when it comes to negative energy. They attract what others feel. This creates an emotional turmoil within them or a psychological imbalance within them. People are more drawn to them since they come across as caring and understanding. Taking the emotional baggage dumped to them, they have a hard time disposing of it. This can be hard on them because the energy remains in their bodies. It makes them come across as depressed, which in some cases they are.

- They are considered to be emotionally weak

Empaths are programmed to be more sensitive humans to the surroundings. They are strong people who walk around carrying the energies of other people.

- Laziness

Empaths may appear to be lazy but that not the case. They have low mental, emotional, and physical energy to the fact that they feel the intense emotions of others. Their minds are overloaded most of the time with the stress, pressure, and tension they have picked up. This translates to being people of low energy but never lazy.

Growing up as an empath in the 21st century can be even tougher due to the stress that comes with this century. It can cause one to not function as healthy empath. The modern habits, including smoking, entertainment, and many more are known to overstimulate the bodies. This can be a negative thing since the more stimulated you are as a person, the more distant you are from yourself. Sometimes having grown up in certain conditions, people tend to send stimuli as a means of escapism. Growing up in a way that one is emotionally dulled emotionally wounded or even growing up in families that shunned away sensitivity, one may learn how to suppress over sensitivity. This can serve as a good thing since you learn how to survive in your surroundings. While you may identify as an empath, it is possible to have blocked overwhelming and negative emotions.

Being able to feel and be who you are makes life easy to live. Blocking empathy abilities isn't as easy as it sounds.

Even when you've blocked your empathic skills, you can reclaim your empathic powers and be able to live fully as an empathic being. The first step is exploring the ways you have used to suppress your sensitivity. You can also try to figure out why you hide from who you are or from your hypersensitivity. You might want to keep a journal and write them down. Face them head on to reclaim your power as an empath.

Being an empath, you might find that consciously allowing yourself to feel discomfort, without being attached to be much healthier, energizing and can lead to psychological balancing. Having empathy can be viewed as having the ability to experience the depth of life without trying too hard to do so. It more of a gift than it is a curse. Embrace it and be able to nurture it in every way possible. It can be a blessing in disguise.

Empaths are able to head to their deepest needs and wants. They are of service to others because of the gift of empathy. As an empath, you are able to see the absolute beauty of life.

In life, you may have encountered a waiter who suggested a better meal on the menu or a salesperson who went out of their way to get you a good deal. You may relate to having a supportive team leader or an executive who doesn't forget your name. The people mentioned above all have one thing in common, and that is they excel in social awareness.

Social Awareness

To have an outstanding quality of social awareness requires you to have empathy, organizational awareness, and a sense of service. Organizational awareness is defined by understanding the politics in an organization's setup and how they affect the people within them. Service usually requires one to be aware and be up to the task in meeting the needs of clients and customers.

In social situations, awareness requires you to anticipate people's wants and to have a plan of communication that is aimed at meeting their specific needs.

I wouldn't go as far as to compare it to manipulation. Manipulation is purposefully calculated to control using unfair means. Social awareness is best at natural. It aims at taking people's situations and needs into consideration as much as possible. Public speakers and great leaders are expected to be socially aware as it goes a long way in gaining the support of the masses.

Caring

Scientific American reported research findings showing a deterioration in levels of empathy, which is our ability to relate to other people's feelings, as compared to how it was thirty years ago. This can be explained by the increase in social isolation in our societies today.

The new forms of digital media have paved the way for digital communication, social networking, and even video conferencing. This means it's no longer necessary for one-on-one interactions, making social isolation more rampant.

It has become easy to be negative to others while socializing online as you don't meet these people face-to-face. This has given rise to a new social menace referred to as cyberbullying. On the other hand, if you don't feel like relating to people's experiences, disengaging is as easy as a touch of a button. You just have to log off or unfriend the person, which is always an easy option.

When paying no attention to the needs and experiences of others, there is bound to be corrosion of trust in society.

If you can't relate to my thoughts and feelings, you are bound to isolate yourself and therefore trust me less. Loss of empathy has significant effects as trust is the cornerstone of successful leadership and partnerships even in business.

Chapter 8: Breaking Free From a Narcissist

Overcoming Loneliness (After Narcissistic Abuse)

Although being with a narcissist is a truly horrific and often traumatic experience, breaking free can lead to initial loneliness. You are so used to being with that person, being involved in their stories, games, and sense of companionship even if it is a twisted and mentally-emotionally abusive companionship; that finally leaving and being free can leave you feeling empty. This is natural- we are all chalices waiting to be filled. We need connections, stories, relationships and various realities to keep us feeling alive and fulfilled. So when you break free from the narcissist you are essentially an empty vessel. *What new stories are you going to create?*

This is of course in itself a beautiful process and fundamentally part of your journey. To be alone is to be all one, content, free and soulfully happy in your on independence. Once we remove attachments and stories which are no longer good for us, we provide ourselves the space and time for new stories; new realities and frequencies of being. I once heard the saying that life is like music. Life can be equated with music. We do live in a *uni*verse after all! So, loneliness can be overcome by filling yourself with new stories- ones in *harmony* with your best interests and best possible expression of you.

Connected to this is a self- recovery, healing and boundary plan. Boundaries are very important, but so is your personal re- discovery of self and self- healing. Below are 5 key and highly effective ways to overcome loneliness.

1. Passion Projects

Immerse yourself in a passion project. New hobbies, favorite pastimes or creating a vision board to align with your dreams and aspirations can all be marvellous gateways back to your true self. Following your greatest joy allows you to overcome loneliness and heal from the sufferings caused by your narcissistic partner. Passion and fire are the spark of life, they re- energize and revitalize your inner core further enabling you to stop feeling isolated or cut off from the world. This is an unfortunate consequence of being the victim of narcissistic abuse or mind manipulations- you may feel disconnected to others on a profound level. Refinding yourself through a passion project is essential for your well- being.

2. Re- Finding Yourself ("Know thyself!")

Have you ever heard of the saying *know thyself?* This is knowing yourself on every level; your intentions, goals, dreams, hidden motivations and your personality in its entirety. We usually become lost and allow in the illusions and judgements of others when we do not know ourselves. 'The self' is the holistic part of being, the persona, characteristics and beliefs which make us unique. It is our thoughts, feelings, subtle impressions, emotions, past experience and deeper inner workings, also having a soulful aspect or significance. Recovering from a narcissist and refinding yourself tie in closely to knowing yourself, or knowing thyself. Not only can taking steps to rediscover and know thyself help you overcome loneliness, it will also help increase your self- esteem, self- worth and personal confidence.

3. Meditation

As briefly delved into earlier meditation is one of the most profound ways to heal from a narcissist. Feeling lonely is due to the feelings of separation or disconnectedness, and these all stem from your mind and emotions. Meditating *reconnects* you to your true self, inner harmony, and a sense of peace and well- being. It also expands your mind and allows you to be an observer of any chaotic, destructive or afflictive thoughts, beliefs or emotions. During the many months or years of narcissistic abuse you will have been through some terrible manipulative treatment. You may have been gaslighted, made to feel small, weak or inferior, or generally insulted on repeat. Your feelings, opinions, and perspectives may have been overlooked and where your beautiful qualities and strengths should have been supported, encouraged and cherished; you instead received neglect and abuse. All in all, your partner knocked your confidence and self- esteem in many unseen ways.

These all have profound negative effects on your inner belief systems, psyche and unconscious workings. Thoughts and emotions, which shape and define you as a person, are strongly influenced by experience and memories; so any abuse you may have suffered can become deeply ingrained. Meditation fills you with a "conscious emptiness," an empty space for new levels of thought, feeling and awareness. You may be able to access your higher self and higher mind, feel better and more positive about your life, and see all negative happenings as an opportunity for growth and new wisdom. In short, feeling lonely is replaced with feeling empowered.

4. Self- Therapy

The importance and power of self- therapy really cannot be undermined or overlooked. Self- therapy- any type of therapy that can be performed at home or in our own time- is great for mind, body, emotions and spirit. It is not just your thoughts and emotions which suffer during narcissistic abuse but also your soul, the core and hidden part of yourself. This is the part that allows us to feel love, empathy, a deeper connection to others and life's beauty; connect with music and access transcendental states, and develop advanced cognitive, intuitive and emotional frequency functioning.

Self- therapy incorporates a wide range of choices and channels so fortunately there is bound to be at least one route which works for you. Meditation, sound therapy, nature therapy, music, art, creative expression, spiritual literature, yoga, tai chi, massage, energy work and mindfulness are all forms of self- therapy. In fact, many people can change their whole mindset through the self- love and care which comes with engaging in therapy. Choosing to give yourself a healing massage, listening to soothing and peaceful music, and going for a mindful walk in nature or reading some soulful poetry can all be effective self -therapies in their own rights.

5. New Social Groups and Organizations

Balanced with all the other key ways to overcome loneliness and heal for the long term is the engagement of new social groups and organizations. This can include peer support, groups for victims of narcissistic abuse, or simply any organization or venture which allows you to feel good. Being happy and connecting with others is the best way to let go and move forward with your life, despite the initial loneliness you may feel. You can feel lonely or isolated in a group too as the truth is- loneliness is just a mindset. Some people feel lonely even when surrounded by family and peers, just as many feel most at peace and blissful when alone. True happiness and contentment comes from your ability to connect and feel at ease with the world. Taking the first steps by putting yourself out there will re-spark your passion for life and connection, and your connection with yourself.

Boundaries: Your New Power Word

Boundaries are your new power word! Breaking free and liberating yourself cannot occur until you put healthy boundaries in place. Not only do they need to be healthy but they need to be strong, so there is no chance of magnetizing or attracting another narcissistic relationship into your orbit.

Let's look at all the ways to create, develop and maintain a boundary plan.

1. Positive Self- Talk and Power Words

Positive self- talk may not initially appear as a form of boundary creating, however it is. Self- talk is the conversations we have with ourselves. When we engage in positive self- talk we open new neural pathways and actively influence the neurons in our brains. These neurons are responsible for the way we think, feel and respond to people, situations and experiences. They are also responsible for our communication, both internal with ourselves and external through our interactions with others. Just through positive and mindful self- talk, a natural boundary is created due to the ripple effect thoughts have on inner and external reality. In short, an invisible energy field is created through the power of the mind, thoughts and subtle intentions exhibited. This invisible energy field is your boundaries.

Connected to this is the effect of power words, specific words used with self- talk to enhance and amplify the power of your boundaries. Words can in fact be used- spoken or thought like a *mantra* or *affirmation* for optimum effect. Neuroscientists have discovered the incredible influence thoughts have on our physical being, emotions and over- all well- being or vibratory state (inner frequency), and this is backed up by a number of other schools of thought. Neuro- linguistic programming, cognitive behavioral therapy, and many alternative therapies and healing modalities all recognize and support the truth that our thoughts are powerful shapers and creators of our world. It is not only inner currents which are affected but worldly reality as we know it. So, harnessing the power of your mind in your boundary goals will allow your personal boundaries to expand and grow stronger, assisting you for the better.

2. Self- Affirmations

Connected to this are self- affirmations, or affirmations. Self- affirmations are essentially affirmations which can be spoken or thought during meditation or any contemplative activity for great effect. They are best performed as a sort of ritual or daily integrated habit. Taking time to dedicate some minutes to affirmations daily will enable your aura, your electromagnetic energy field to be strengthened and expanded and your mind strengthened. As the body is a complex and interconnected system, this has a profound effect on your emotions and thus increases your sense of boundaries on many levels. Mental boundaries, emotional boundaries, physical boundaries and spiritual boundaries are real, and once you begin to truly develop your own boundaries you will realize how 'one and the same' these all are. Once you strengthen one of your boundary muscles you can protect yourself from harmful or destructive energy. This includes the intentions and attempted projections of your narcissistic ex!

To engage in self- affirmations in an effective way, make time for a daily morning and/ or evening routine. This routine creates a structure in your life and an almost 'ceremonial' aspect. This is precisely what affirmations are, a sort of ceremony like meditation. Setting your intentions and committing to self- affirmations as a daily routine inevitably sharpens and strengthens your mind, further opening you up to new ways of perceiving. Included in this is protecting yourself and the connection this morning or evening routine has to self- healing and your aura.

3. Self- Healing/ Aura Strengthening

Kirlian photography has shown how there is an electromagnetic energy field surrounding each one us known as an aura to some. Spiritual beings, healers and energy workers have been aware of this energy field or aura for quite some time, however it is only in recent years where the science to support it has made itself known. All living entities have an electromagnetic energy field, from plants to animals and homo sapiens. This energy field is responsible for all thoughts, feelings, subtle impressions, beliefs, interactions, emotions, past memories and experiences, and one's general energy and vibration. We give off vibrations in every moment, and this is where the modern age term "vibes" has originated from. In terms of kirlian photography, one's aura can be seen to show just how real subtle energy and influences are. Science recognizes this 'invisible circle' responsible for our sense of boundaries as an electromagnetic energy field, whereas spiritual people and communities call it an aura. The term used is a technicality and regardless of your personal beliefs, what matters is the powerful and positive effects strengthening your aura has on your ability to protect yourself from the harm of narcissists. (Both the one currently leaving your life and all future ones.)

How do you strengthen your aura, you may be wondering? Self-healing is the key and fortunately there are many ways to do this. Meditation, engaging in therapy- either self- therapy or through seeking the help of others, and any sort of spiritual or healing activities and practices can all help you develop strong boundaries through aura-strengthening. There is so much guidance available nowadays through both Youtube and the internet and in presence, through teachers, workshops and practitioners experienced and qualified in their fields. Doing your own research at which route, if any, may be best for you may just be the secret missing ingredient to your perfected boundary plan. Many people are awakening to the spirit which flows through all living things and to our own spiritual power, and recognizing that the scientific electromagnetic energy field is in fact a powerful and very real aura! A boundary plan would not be complete without this aspect.

4. Physical Movement and Exercise: Strength

Strength is a key factor in your ability to be centered and aligned within. This alignment is to your own truth, self- respect and personal empowerment, which all come with strong and healthy boundaries. Physical movement and exercise strengthen you physically and with a strong body comes a strong character. The mind, body and spirit are designed to work in harmony, so improving your physical fitness and stamina has a positive effect on your character, willpower and mental-emotional boundaries. When you feel strong and centered through physical exercise you also feel more assertive, positive and deserving-deserving all life has to offer. This means you will *not* accept the ill-treatment or manipulations of a narcissistic ex you have fought so hard to separate from. Physical vitality, fitness and health inevitably makes you stronger, and this means you can put up better boundaries.

5. Emotional Muscles

Strengthening and developing your emotional muscles must be part of your boundary plan. Your emotional resilience, intelligence and connection are your keys to success. Empathy, intuition and an advanced to mature emotional connection to both yourself and others (the world around) allows you to stay centered within and aligned to your truth, own reality and choice to stay clear from narcissistic abuse, and the games of your ex. Emotions can be seen as a muscle, even if figuratively as they control and shape all of physical reality as we know it. We are essentially emotional creatures and those who are in tune with their inner empath (advanced empathy) or higher frequency functioning emotions can, literally, influence others and reality in a powerful and positive way.

Let's briefly look at the qualities associated with and necessary for a boundary plan with regard to developing and strengthening your emotional muscles.

Emotional Resilience

Emotional resilience allows you to adapt and respond to stressful or chaotic situations with ease and poise or grace. Your emotional health is strong and you know yourself well enough to not react. Life's difficulties and challenges can be overcome easily if not effortlessly based on the way you can recover, adapt and change with the tides.

Emotional Intelligence

Emotional intelligence is the capacity to be aware of and in control of your emotions. You can easily express yourself and possess a certain wisdom and empathy to you which reflects in your interactions and communications. Interpersonal relationships can be handled judiciously, fairly and maturely and you often shine light on others and situations. Emotional intelligence is a key trait to possess when dealing with a narcissist, specifically during the break- up and letting go period.

Empathy

Empathy allows you to possess all of the other key characteristics as to be empathetic is to literally feel what it is like to be another, or be in another's shoes. This allows you to deal with difficulties or strenuous interactions (with your narcissistic ex) in a way that is compassionate, self- respecting and wise. Possessing empathy and seeking ways to develop it allows you to increase your own boundaries, making them stronger through your ability to connect with a higher frequency (compassion, patience, empathetic- related qualities, etc).

Intuition

Intuition is your guiding light and your inner compass. It is also known as your gut or gut feeling, and can tell you which path to take or not to take in moments of need. It is also responsible for your instincts, instinctual awareness, your emotional wisdom, and your ability to know and follow your truth. Intuition connects you to a higher wisdom and awareness and to your seat of personal power- those strongly connected to their intuition know what to say and when, how to act and respond in each moment, and generally everything that will keep them on course. What better way to enhance and expand your boundaries than to develop, and connect to, your intuition?

Emotional Independence

Emotional independence is a sure way to develop and maintain boundaries. Acquiring this sets you apart from the entanglement you once suffered at the hands of your narcissist other (partner). When you are emotionally independent you have greater if not a certain chance of being free from mind games, manipulations, narcissistic entrapments and the general dark motivations and intentions of your ex.

6. Connecting to Your Spiritual Source

Finally, connecting to your spiritual source should be part of any boundary plan. The extent of this will differ for everyone individually, as everyone will have their own limits and be on their own journey. Spiritual source can mean many things to many different people; to some it can be as intense as spending days to weeks on a mountain meditating to a state of deep spiritual enlightenment. To others it may be recognizing spirit which runs through all of life and every living thing. The fundamental point is that connecting to spirituality or your own 'inner spirit', in any way, can have a profound effect on your personal strength. Boundaries come from strength and opening yourself up spiritually can make you mentally, emotionally or physically stronger too.

Chapter 9: What are Covert Narcissists?

Have you ever encountered a person who started of as being your colleague, friend or partner who would listen to you, help you and cheer for you, only to realize, months, even years later that they never really cared for your wellbeing the whole time? Someone who you believed was on your team but turned out to be the person who, as the time went by made you feel guilty, drained or as if you are not good, or attractive enough? If not, then you are the lucky one. If yes, you are a strong person who has dealt with, or suspects are dealing with something psychiatrists call a covert narcissist.

Covert narcissism is a Cluster B personality disorder that describes a person who exhibits a series of recognizable narcissistic traits, with some of the most distinctive ones being the lack of empathy for others and quiet superiority. Although it has roots in childhood, the first signs are showing as the disorder develops in late teens and early twenties, after which it continues to progress. To really understand what this means, it's important to dive into what a narcissistic behavior really is at its core first, as all subcategories of narcissism, including covert narcissism, revolve around the same personality traits.

Some might say a narcissist is a person who loves themselves a bit too much. And while this is true, when it comes to this personality disorder, things are not that simple. In popular culture, narcissism is usually associated with a group of personality traits, such as extreme self-centeredness, grandiose sense of self, one's achievements and looks. But, in psychiatric practice, this phenomenon goes a lot deeper than an inflated sense of self-importance. The main reason why it is so hard to spot a narcissist and define one lies in the fact that that there is not only one parametre by which a narcissist can be defined but a few distinctive parameters. So, what is narcissistic personality disorder all about? Psychiatrists look for these traits:

- If someone in your environment seems to pay attention only to how they feel, discarding everyone else's opinions, feelings and thoughts, you might be dealing with a narcissist. A narcissist has a lack of empathy for others and takes into consideration only their needs and wants.

- A person who is willing to achieve their goals at all costs, even if that means manipulating others or disrespecting their boundaries to get what they want can possibly be a narcissist. Their primary focus is on themselves, and themselves only.

- Someone with a narcissistic personality disorder often indulges in daydreaming about having all the power and, being high above everyone else, instead of being equal with others. This is frequently followed by the firm belief that they deserve nothing but the best and nothing below perfect suits them, b.3 social status, career, romantic partner or a group of friends.

- Because they are ''above everyone else'', narcissists tend to think that they are entitled to be treated as such. They see themselves as special, and deem others as average, not good enough or below their league. Naturally, such an individual is often described as arrogant which is evident in the way how they treat others. Everyone who doesn't like them is, in their eyes, envious and hateful, as they are not as nearly beautiful, talented or successful as the narcissist is.

•   A narcissist desires approval and wants to be admired no matter how big their achievements are. Matter effect, they want to be recognized as superior even when that superiority has no firm foundation in reality. If someone in your circle expects to be recognized as the most talented, the most beautiful or the most successful person no matter whether that is objectively true or not, you might be dealing with a narcissist.

Not all of the above are equally present in a narcissist's behavior and persona, as there are different levels and types we can speak of. While in some more severe cases all of these are very noticeable, in most cases it takes some time and expertise to diagnose one as a narcissist. When it comes to types, there are few classifications out there, with the most narrow being the one given by James F. Masterson, which differentiates narcissists in two categories: the exhibitionist and closet subtypes. The exhibitionist subtype is the so-called ''extraverted'', overt narcissist, the one that we think of when someone mentions the word narcissist - the person who seems to tick all the above-mentioned boxes of personality traits, as they openly display them. Frequently, with overt narcissists, what you see is what you get. With covert types, this is far from the truth.

Hiding behind the mask of sensitive, empathetic types that care for others and their wellbeing, closet narcissists also believe they are important and special just like overts do, but unlike their extraverted brothers, don't show it openly. Because overts usually have open displays of their own grandiosity, it takes less time to see their narcissistic traits and therefore leaves them behind. With coverts, this game looks a bit different. In many cases, they appear to be quite the opposite of what a movie version of a narcissist looks like, which is why it may take years for them to be recognized as such. All that there is in our classic, overt narcissist, exists in the second type as well. The difference is in the expression of pathological traits.

What they have in common, and what is related to their lack of empathy, is how they view other people. Not only do they believe they are superior and better than everyone else, but they see people as sources or supplies for their narcissistic needs. Because their self revolves around the belief that they are superior, powerful and worth admiring, they, as such, need an audience to cheer for them, like a star needs their fans to thrive in the world of celebrities. A narcissist, no matter the type, thinks as a predator and you are their prey.

Both overt and covert narcissists are damaging to people they associate with. Both exhibit narcissistic traits and both have a lack of empathy and all other traits common for this disorder. However, here is the catch - covert types are the narcissists in disguise. And that is where their power for destruction lies. Matter effect, these types are those that have the most devastating effect on other's well being, solely for the fact that they are not easy to spot. Most of the time, it is quite the opposite.

Socially acceptable, people who others usually respect and believe are the ones that can offer support and guidance is just the role they are playing. And better believe it, they rehearsed it many, many times. It is a skill they have mastered because they know the best way to get what they want from others is by making others feel safe around them. Once you meet them, you will rarely get red flags you'd get with the other type as they know very well how negatively people can react to the open displays of arrogance or superiority.

These individuals, deep down believe they are special and better than everyone they have ever met, but somehow, the world overlooks their uniqueness and above-average qualities. But you won't see them blurting about it. Not in the beginning stages of your relationship with them. They actually care what you think of them. But not because they want to impress you and truly care for you, but because they need you to approve them. And trust me, they will go the distance to get this approval. They need to feel validated and the best way to do that is by making you feel like you are important, talented, listened to, cared for and understood - which is exactly what *they* need from you.

Still not sure how this game works? It might comfort you to know that even many psychiatrists get carried away by their charm in the initial stages of psychotherapy - that is if they ever get to therapy.

By making you feel safe, important, praised and appreciated, they by themselves a seat in your group of friends or associates. What they give you in the first months or years of knowing them is exactly what they want from you and what they will demand you to give them later on. Their attention and appreciation of you in the first stage is their way of ensuring a narcissistic supply. But, because of their ways of ensuring such a supply, after the *love bombing stage,* their supplies, people who are their targets

The real danger of encountering them lies in the fact that they act like someone you'd love to have in your life. They are kind, dedicated, cheer for you and know how to make you feel special, so who wouldn't want them in their life? This is their mastery of charm, that will, however, be present throughout all stages of a relationship with them. In the beginning, they will use it to win you over and by the end, they will use this charm to turn yourself against someone you should love and trust the most - yourself. This is when this allure joins with another trait of theirs used to control their supply, and that is passive-aggressiveness which becomes the main tool for gaslighting, a process we are yet to decode in the text that follows.

What is common for victims of narcissistic abuse, especially for those who have suffered the abuse from a covert narcissist, is low self-esteem, guilt, shame, poor self-image, despair, depression, anxiety, self-doubt, insomnia, trust issues, isolation, and even paranoia. In the majority of cases, the narcissist was someone very close to the victim, such as a parent, a sibling or their best friend, which is why having one in your life can be so devastating. These are the people who were supposed to always have your back. Unfortunately, sometimes that is not the truth.

If everything you have read so far sounds too familiar to you, I hope it brings you relief to know that what you have experienced or are experiencing is not something you are imagining. You are not going crazy. You have been gaslighted as every victim of narcissistic abuse is. It might comfort you to know that you were chosen by them as you are a worthy supply, not because you are worthless, crazy, oversensitive, unattractive or anything else they made you believe you are once the bliss of the initial stage of relationship with them fizzled out. What you need to know is that narcissists pick their victims only if the victim has something to offer, be it your optimism, intelligence, empathy, status, money or your good looks that they used to show you around. Or all of the above.

Many who are or have been in a relationship with such a damaging individual lived or live in the state of denial because covert narcissists are manipulators of the first class, and will twist the mind even of the most intelligent person. So don't beat yourself up. You are not alone in this and we will bust the covert together, understand who they are, but most importantly focus on you and how you can heal from such toxic energy only a closer narcissist can bring into your life.

In the book, I will use the terms victim, target and a survivor to describe someone who has been or is dealing with a narcissist. A victim and a target, because that is how the narcissist sees their supplies and survivor because that is what people who had experienced narcissistic abuse truly are. Brave people who unfortunately had to cross paths with these toxic individuals and fight for keeping their light shining even in the darkest times.

Take a breather and let's decode them so you can understand what kind of individual you were dealing with. Here we go.

Chapter 10:   The Abuse Cycle

The Narcissistic Abuse Cycle

Many times, the victim will know because of their logical mind that the narcissist is toxic and abusive. However, the emotions will come into play, thanks to the work of the narcissist, and the victim will start doubting reality. They will stay in the relationship, mainly because they are so willing to follow their heart, rather than seeing what the situation is. if there are higher traits of codependency with the victim, the option of leaving will seem super painful, so the victim will stay.

There are five phases that are present in the abuse cycle. These are all connected together, and they need to be present for the victim to be caught with the abuser for longer than they should. The parts that come with the abuse cycle include:

Idealize

The first part of the abuse cycle is idealizing. This will make it so that the narcissist will appear better than who they are. When we enter this stage, the narcissist will do a process that is known as love bombing. This means that they will try and create an ideal relationship for the victim. They do this by showing tons of affection, love, and interest. This will lead the victim to feel a deep sense of trust to the narcissist, and can make the victim feel like they and the narcissist are connecting on a deeper level.

The victim will feel like they are in love here. They will try and share many things with the narcissist, letting go of their deepest secrets, fears, and hopes. The narcissist may appear to be sharing information as well but it is rarely genuine and often it isn't even the truth.

Devalue

Once the narcissist is sure that the victim is hooked and invested in the relationship, it is time for the narcissist to move to the devaluation phase. This is when they will take some time to chip away at the perceptions of the victim, making even the strengths of the victim look like flaws. This will be a slow process going from idealization to devaluation. The narcissist knows that if they make the switch too much, they will end up scaring you off. There will be small little changes, ones that are almost impossible to see, so that the victim stays around.

The narcissist will start with all pull and no push, reeling the victim in and ensuring that they will come back for more. Over time, this will start changing. There is first ten percent, then twenty percent, and then thirty percent, and so on. The narcissist will increase based on the victim's tolerance for the abuse when it gets started. if someone comes in with low boundaries to start, then the narcissist will move through the process a bit faster. But they may move at a slower rate if they are dealing with someone who comes in with stronger boundaries.

Discard

As the devaluation phase gets worse, the victim is likely to become desperate here. They want to make sure that they can get themselves back to the idealization phase where they felt good. But during these attempts, the narcissist will discard their victim. Because the victim is dealing with feeling insignificant and insecure, the narcissist knows that the victim will do anything to seek their approval. This will condition the victim to seek excessive admiration from the narcissist, which gives them more control.

It is common during this time for the narcissist to withdraw, telling their victim that everything they have done for them is a sign of failure, and they will blame the victim for not making them feel good. This causes the victim to blame themselves when things don't go right. As the victim still continues to try and seek validation in a desperate manner, the narcissist will use these attempts as they way that they seek their praise, admiration, attention, and validation. While the victim is trying to get back on the good side of the narcissist and they are trying to keep themselves happy, they are fueling the fire and are not giving the narcissist a reason to be nice.

Destroy

When we get to this phase, there is a strong possibility that the other relationships that the narcissist has been working on have now developed a bit more than before. The narcissist will have more than one source of narcissistic supply, and it is likely that they will become less dependent on that one victim.

During this phase, the narcissist will put more pressure on the victim to take all the blame. They will dig more into the devaluation process, using all of the vulnerability and weakness as a chance to drive the abuse down deep. They will switch back and forth between these two phases with the victim, which makes that victim feel like they are worthless and that they have nowhere to go. The narcissist will make this worse because they will make the victim feel like they should leave because they are no longer welcome.

Many of the victims who are at this stage feel like they don't even have the strength to walk away, and it seems impossible to undo all of the pain and the hurt that is inside of them. The victim will seek out the narcissist as their remedy, even though they may also withdraw a bit because they are scared of being hurt or of the narcissist lashing out at them again. This is a very uncomfortable phase where the victim needs to get the validation of the narcissist but they may feel that it hurts too much to talk to them even.

During the destroy phase, the narcissist will take some time to try and make their victim seem unwanted and unworthy by everyone. They won't just use phrases that show their displeasure in this person. Perhaps they will say something like "No wonder your mother doesn't like having you over anymore" or "This is why your friends don't hang out with you anymore." This makes it seem like the victim doesn't have anywhere else to turn. Even though the narcissist is the reason that those people quit interacting with you, the narcissist can turn this around and make it seem like you are the one to blame.

Hoover

Once the narcissist is done with the destroy phase, and the victim can get away from the relationship for a bit, then the victim and the narcissist are likely to spend some of their time apart. For a bit, it may seem like the narcissist has stopped and you are abandoned for now. If you are coming out of this phase for the first time, know that this is not done. The narcissist may have some other victims that they are working with as well, these are the back up. It is likely that they are not done with the first victim.

The hoover phase is one where a lot of the trauma will happen, even though the rest of the cycle will be traumatic and exhausting as well.

Here, the victim is not able to fight their addiction, or the need that they have for validation. Some may be able to escape the narcissist for a few weeks, and maybe even for a few months but most will end up returning.

Soon, the victim, wishing for the relationship to go back to the way that it was, will start idealizing the relationship in their mind. They miss that person, the narcissist, so they will learn how to ignore all of the bad and the negative experiences, and will just focus on the positive ones. They will romanticize that idealization phase, while hiding the rest. After enough time has passed, the narcissist knows that the victim will be able to downplay the abuse in their heads. And this is the perfect time for the narcissist to come back.

Feels Threatened

When your abuser discovers you have left the relationship, they most certainly will have a response. How much of that response you have to see will depend on how much distance you can put between you and how strong the shields you've set up prove to be.

In an ideal world, you would never have to talk to them again. Unfortunately, the real world is messy and you likely have shared friends, shared hangout spots and your abuser knows your habits and thus the best time and place to catch you off guard.

The good news is that your abuser's attention may wane more quickly
Though you've taken away their "toy" and their ego
abuser has a narcissistic personality then
they are simply not capable of forming deep
hey cannot love to the same depths that a

"normal" person can love and thus they will not take as long to move on.

They may even threaten self-harm, an extreme attempt to force you to talk to them and perhaps force you back into the relationship. If this happens, you could not be blamed for worrying – you are human, you thus have compassion. Not to mention that this is a person you love or loved. However, remember that your return to the relationship would not solve a psychological problem that led to threats of suicide. Even in a healthy relationship, you would enlist help for them.

So instead of allowing them to manipulate you, call 911. Allow the proper authorities who are trained to intervene in a suicidal situation to take over – that is what they are for. Don't feel guilty for doing this rather than giving your abuser what they want. If the breakup has made them suicidal, they need this help. It would be the right thing to do in any circumstance.

Abuses Others

The Manipulator Who Uses Guilt

The manipulator who makes you take a guilt trip is, perhaps, one of the most dangerous gaslighting practitioners in the world. Here are some classic statements the 'guilt builders' employ on their victims:

- If you were a good child, you would listen to your mama.
- If you truly loved me, you would not say no.
- If you really understood what I have gone through, you would not speak to me like this.
- **If you were a good husband, you would never refuse my request.**

They fill the victims' minds with self-guilt and make them pli
Then, such guilt builders enforce their main ideas and the

highly vulnerable victim. Nothing works like guilt to turn on a repenting attitude, and manipulators want their victims to show repentance so that they can use it to their advantage.

What happens when you repent? It means you are sorry and are prepared for punishment, which is a perfect situation for them to start controlling you and your mind. Such manipulators blame you for all the wrong things, including their own behavior. For example, 'If you hadn't said that nasty thing, I would not have behaved as badly as I did.' So, their bad behavior becomes your problem.

The ones who cannot take responsibility for anything in their lives are the ones who typically use guilt building tactic to control others. This kind of manipulative behavior is based primarily on emotionally weak people who are ready to take responsibility for real and imagined faults to be accepted by the manipulator.

Manipulators who use guilt tend to carry their emotional scars like a badge showing it off to everyone so that they can control the people around them. Here are some common words or situations used by this type of manipulator to make you guilty:

- I have had such a bad childhood.
- You don't know the amount of pain I went through looking after my sick father.
- I have had to put up with your horrible father, and you simply don't know what I have sacrificed for your sake.
- **You are angry because I am not ready for commitment. But, you don't know how difficult it is for me considering that I suffered loneliness after my father abandoned me.**

The Aggressive Manipulator or 'Threatener'

The most common forms of abuse perpetrated by the aggressive or threatening kind of manipulator is domestic abuse. Here are some classic lines that this kind of manipulator will spew from his or her mouth:

- I will beat you black and blue if you don't give me the money.
- I will kill you if you don't listen to me.
- I will throw you onto the streets if you don't heed my words.
- **I will not give you food if you don't complete your homework on time.**

People who have a lot of physical and mental strength generally tend to use this kind of manipulation tactic. They are confident of the fear they can instill in the victim using whichever method they can to get their work done. The 'threatener' will threaten to destroy your career, family, relationships, and more.

'Threateners' are great blackmailers who tend to take advantage of the secret information they have on others to control people. The thing about this type of manipulator is that they may be strong physically, and yet, they lack the courage to do things in the open. They tend to hide their aggressive behavior and will display it only in front of their victims and no one else.

The deep sense of fear created by 'threateners' can be powerful enough to drive victims to do their bidding,the including getting gaslighted. 'Threateners' also tend to isolate their victims from supportive family and friends. Being isolated like this makes victims surrender themselves entirely to the mercy of 'threateners.'

The most evident sense of fear is rooted in being physically abused by this type of manipulator. It is imperative that you do everything in your power to steer clear of such manipulators as their aggression can lead to fatality too.

While the physical threat is one way to manipulate, subtle forms of threats are also employed by manipulators. For example, a wife who wants to control her husband's diet might say, 'If you continue to eat this way, you can rest assured that in less than six months, you will look at a huge drum.' Here, the wife wants to control the eating habits of her husband. She uses this threat as a way of controlling one aspect of her husband's life. It's likely that the wife hates to see her husband's happy face when he eats and wants to wipe that pleasure from his life.

The Manipulator Who Uses the Silent Treatment

The ones who are not smart enough to get you on a guilt trip or be aggressive tend to use the silent treatment to manipulate. This type of manipulation is most effective when you, as the victim, desperately need the help of the manipulator. Such manipulative techniques withdraw all kinds of communication and contact with the victim until their desires are achieved.

When it comes to romantically involved partners, then this type of manipulator will withdraw even sex from the equation. In fact, women manipulators tend to play this card to control their male partners knowing full well that some men need sex like food and water!

A silent treatment manipulation is a powerful form of emotional abuse as it negatively affects the very basic need of human beings to be in touch with others. The silent treatment is meant to instill a fear of getting disconnected with the manipulator in the minds of the victims. It is also generally used by people in the initial stages of romantic relationships. The controlling partner would have used charm and fake compassion to build the necessary connection, and then turn on the silent treatment to start and deepen the controlling effect.

When faced with the silent treatment suddenly, the victim feels the fear of rejection and abandonment and will do anything to win back favor with the manipulator. The silent treatment giver can result in utterly frustrating the victim. There are many reasons why people use the silent treatment method, including:

- It makes them take the 'high moral road' giving them the upper hand in any relationship.
- Other methods of showing their displeasure have not produced their desired outcomes.
- **It is easy to defend this kind of behavior later on. All that needs to be said is, 'I said nothing,' and wash off all blame and accountability in the relationship.**

Examples, where silent treatment manipulators work effectively are:

- A mother ignoring her child
- Silent treatment on online platforms
- Nonverbal show of anger like throwing things randomly
- **Keeping a colleague out of a collaborative project**

The Manipulator Who Attacks Your Self-Esteem

This type of manipulator attacks your self-esteem by:

- Putting you down
- Labeling you
- Passing judgments
- **Showing contempt**

The self-esteem attackers do everything they can to criticize you and make you feel inferior. The worst thing is that these verbal attacks need not be direct. If someone tells you, "Only working women wear lipstick during the day,' it translates to telling you that you are a whore, doesn't it?

Conclusion

How you interact with your family, friends, colleagues, and romantic partners largely depends on your social skills. However, if you want to build good social skills, empathy is one of the things to incorporate.

Empathy is defined as "the ability to acknowledge and share the feelings and experience of another person." In the way of explanation, it is expressed as putting yourself on someone else shoes, feel and understand what they go through and see yourself and the rest of the world from their point of view. You can't understand why someone did whatever he did or act a certain way until you imagine yourself in his or her position, walk in his or her skin and consider things from his or her perspective.

Being an empath does not end the moment you finally found yourself. In fact, a more exciting life is just about to start right there. Once you fully embrace yourself, things will start falling into place. Only then will you realize that what you have in you is a gift. And you will be able to use that gift properly at your own will.

However, just because you can control your ability doesn't mean you are immune to exhaustion and meltdown. Always keep in your mind that you are an empath and you are meant to respond sensitively to energies around you. Because of that, you will be needing strategies to maintain balance whenever you run into draining situations. Even the skilled and strongest empaths out there know that they need to recharge themselves every once in a while. So, adopt their winning mindset and keep these recharging strategies in your mind to make yourself ready for any moments in life, even for the exhausting ones.

Take Micro Breaks

Micro breaks are healthy pauses that usually last 30 seconds to five minutes. As an empath, you battle not only with physically demanding tasks everyday but also with emotional energies that try to enter you. Because of that, you tend to receive more pressure than others. Use these micro breaks to temporarily distract you from work pressure and stress. They can also help you retain focus by relaxing your mind for a while and taking away unnecessary thoughts from it. These short breaks can make a huge difference when it comes to your health and productivity. Empaths who work for straight hours and push themselves beyond limits often end up destroying their health instead of being productive, while empaths who use micro breaks, though slower, usually maintain a steady working pace and a healthy flow of energy in their body.

Focus Your Energy on Your Importance

Keep your energies focused on your importance as it will not only establish a positive mindset, but will also protect you from unwanted forces that may negatively influence your actions and decisions. Through this, you will also learn how to appreciate yourself more. Your self-worth and your self-esteem are important to maintain a balanced flow of energy within you. Always keep the flow of your energy smooth and relaxed so you can control it more easily and appropriately, even when you are bombarded with a lot of negative forces from your external environment.

www.ingramcontent.com/pod-product-compliance
Lightning Source LLC
Chambersburg PA
CBHW051211250726
48655CB00006B/2358